JOHN THE BELIE

Jesus told them this:

"If you were blind you would not be astray; but, as it is, you claim that you can see and you're as much astray as ever."

John 9:41

The Four Gospels
Translated by Norman Marrow

John
The Believable Gospel

Ben Barman

Published by  Friendly Press

300 Gloucester Road
BRISTOL BS7 8PD
England

Order and dispatch address:

Friendly Press (JBG)
White Willows
Littleton-on-Severn
BRISTOL BS12 1NR
England

Set by the author in Lucida Bright typeface.
Printed by SHORT RUN PRESS, Exeter, England

FOREWORD

This is an unusual book. It is not written for biblical scholars though it draws on and draws together the results of scholarship. Nor is it a Bible Study. It is an attempt by an intelligent layman to find out the answers to the questions which troubled him, and then to share the results with others who have the same questions.

Ben Barman's excitement at his discoveries and his enthusiasm for the search shine through every page. As I read the text I shared that excitement, even when I did not agree with the position taken. Ben Barman has not felt constrained by the boundaries of Biblical Studies but has made connections with the life of the spirit and of faith. But most of all he has gone to the historical background of Jesus and tried to show what he was saying and doing and what he meant, in a clear and fresh way.

Ben Barman tells me that some years ago on a Greyhound bus travelling in the U.S.A. I encouraged him to write this book. I am glad I did. I hope that you enjoy it too.

Janet Scott
Homerton College
Cambridge

v

PREFACE

The biblical quotations have been drawn from the Revised Version of the Bible which was translated toward the end of the last century introducing 'as few alterations as possible to the Text of the Authorised Version'. This older wording conveys a sense of poetry and spiritual values which can be obscured by some of the modern translations. Furthermore, the Revised Version follows the original Greek closely giving both a feeling of continuity with the past and also enabling any problems of translation to be brought out. Because the language is sometimes unclear to those coming to it for the first time modifications have been made. Those words which are not in use today have been changed, but words and phrases which are easily understood have been left in even at the expense of grammatical correctness.

The quotations from Josephus, also translated in the 19th century, have been modified in the same way.

The translation in the frontispiece is from Norman Marrow, *The Four Gospels* by permission of the author. The Paul Tillich quote on page 121 is by permission of the Oxford University Press, and the quotation from D Parker-Rhodes, *The Way Out is the Way In* is by permission Quaker Home Service London. The chart on page v adapted from J.A.T.Robinson, *The Priority of John* by permission of SCM Ltd. I am grateful for being allowed to use this material.

This work would not have been possible without the help from many friends who cheerfully listened to my expositions and pointed the way forward with good advice. In particular I am much indebted to those who spent a significant amount of time in reading the manuscript, either in it's very early stage or in it's final form, and making so many positive comments. Among those who have given great support are Tony Brown, The Reverend Gavin Fargus, Robin Hodgkin, Nick Large, Marjorie Nash, Cyril Poster, Jim Pym, Jean Roberts and in particular my dear wife Candia. She has for many years patiently coped with my being immersed in the work and also devoted many hours to guiding and upholding me when the going was difficult.

The views and conclusions of this book are a result of considerable study and reflection and are mine, as are any errors for which I take full responsibility.

Ben Barman
March 1994

CONTENTS

Part 1
SETTING THE SCENE

Part 2
THE STORY OF JESUS AS TOLD BY JOHN

MAJOR CHARTS AND TABLES

THE HOLY LAND

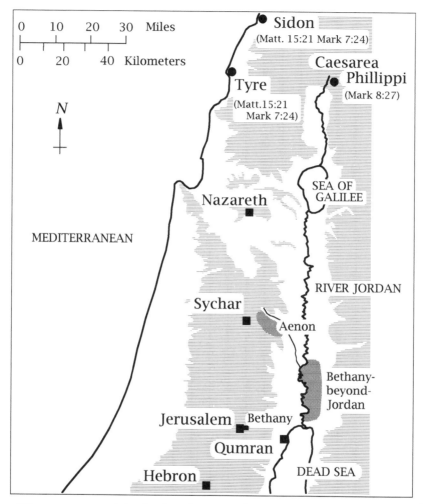

The towns visited by Jesus when attempting to travel unrecognised are marked with a circle:- ●

The places where John the Baptist may have been baptising are shown by the dark areas. The exact location of both Aenon (John 3:23) and Bethany-beyond-Jordan (John 1:28) are unknown.

THE MINISTRY OF JESUS – A TIME SCALE SHOWING PLACES VISITED AND SOME MAJOR EVENTS BASED ON THE FOURTH GOSPEL

31 AD	Feb		? Baptism of Jesus	John 1:29
	Mar	CANA		
	Apr	JERUSALEM for Passover	Temple cleansing	John 2:14
	May		Baptist arrested, Temptation	Matt 4:12 & 4:1
	June		Woman of Samaria	John 4:1
	July			
	Aug	GALILEE		
	Sep			
	Oct	JERUSALEM New Year Tabernacles	Healing at Bethesda 5 colonnades	John 5:1
	Nov			
	Dec		Death of John the Baptist	Matt 14:12
32 AD	JAN	GALILEE		
	Feb			
	Mar		Desert feeding before Passover	John 6:1
	Apr		"Proclaim him King"	John 6:15
	May			
	June			
	July	TYRE, SIDON & GALILEE		Mark 7:24,31
	Aug			
	Sep			
	Oct	JERUSALEM for Tabernacles		John 7:2
	Nov	JUDAEA on the road	Temple police attempt arrest "nowhere to lay his head"	John 7:46 Luke 9:58–10:24
	Dec	JERUSALEM for Dedication	"one more attempt to seize him"	John 10:22–39
33 AD	JAN	BETHANY-BEYOND-JORDAN		John 10:40
	Feb	BETHANY-IN-JUDAEA	The raising of Lazarus	John 11:17
	Mar	EPHRAIM	Jesus a 'wanted' man in hiding	John 11:54
	Apr	JERUSALEM	CRUCIFIXION	John 12:12 John 19:17

The first part of the ministry, to May 31 AD, is partly an extension of the John the Baptist movement with an Old Testament outlook. Following the imprisonment of John the Baptist and the Temptation crises, the story of the Woman of Samaria takes place which epitomises the New Testament ministry.

INTRODUCTION

Of the four gospels in the New Testament it is the last, the Fourth Gospel, —the Gospel of John— that has become the favourite of so many. Beside being the 'spiritual gospel' it is the most intriguing. It has hidden meanings which work at several levels. It has many mysteries; who wrote it, why is it so different from the other gospels? By understanding the complex circumstances at the time of Jesus the story and message which John tells comes to life. That is why this book came into being.

Three family friends of ours from different church backgrounds admitted in confidence that they felt doubtful about God and some of the teaching they had received. "You would be shocked if I told you what I really felt", "I can't pass on to my children what I have been told I must believe", and "The very word God makes me curl up" they said. Yet all were, and still are, deeply spiritual, in touch with God and still held membership of their Church. Each knew that, in some way, he or she was on the right path, but felt out of tune with what was being said by many religious people. Much of the difficulty was in the different interpretation of words.

I can understand. Many years ago I felt the same and, on reading the New Testament, found that it was meaningless. It did not add up in an historical way, and to make matters worse, many of the answers given to the questions asked at school did not make sense. It is important to look at the reasons behind things before understanding and accepting them. What was being taught did not ring true, yet behind all the muddle the message of Jesus somehow shone through.

Some years ago at a short course on Biblical studies (Biblical study is about how and who wrote the Bible; Bible study is about its message) it was explained that modern research, including important discoveries such as the Dead Sea Scrolls, has increased our understanding of what life was like during the time of Jesus. Using this new material the events in the Bible made more and more sense as time went on, even if the conclusions did not follow the traditional viewpoint.

Exploring and discovering are enjoyable. To find out that you

1

were wrong can be refreshing, especially if you take life as an adventure. In this way Biblical and Bible studies are exciting. When you unearth a new fact it is as if the sun suddenly shines. The black patches which were depressingly dark light up, and the whole scene changes. Doubts become certainties and certainties become grey and shadowy, needing further thought.

The views in this book are mine, reflecting how I understand the New Testament. They may be right for me, but that does not necessarily make them right for you. We were created differently, see things in different ways and, as we were created in the image of God these differences are somehow God-sent. Certainly differences and debate keep us from becoming smug and self-satisfied.

Over the years there has been a continual stream of archaeological finds. These finds, such as remains of buildings and graves, have increased our knowledge about the people of the New Testament but there are still many gaps. For instance, it would be interesting to know more about the different religious groups, particularly the Sadducees.

Most of the documented information about the Jewish way of life during the time of Jesus comes from three sources.

1) The Bible,
2) The Jewish historian Josephus,
3) The Dead Sea Scrolls.

Both the New Testament and Josephus' works were written well after the life of Jesus, between 30 and 70 years, and the writers had a particular story to tell which quite naturally they told in the way they understood it. In other words, first-hand evidence is sparse, and most of the evidence relies on the testimony of others which might, or might not, be correct. The authors were reporting what they thought others had said and done, and we do not know how much they were looking at things in their own way.

A difficulty arises for us today when we try to be rational. We cannot but help being emotionally involved when we study the Bible no matter what views we hold. The evidence on which we build our cases easily gets distorted by our prejudices. We tend to pick out only the bits with which we feel most comfortable as being true and to ignore the others. We make a rut for ourselves and find that it becomes a trench getting deeper and deeper as

2

we interpret more and more of the evidence in our own particular way. Often that evidence is based on previous evidence which has also been so interpreted.

In our considerations we think we are being scientific and objective but in reality we make many subjective choices. Sometimes the judgement of an outsider without a preconceived framework turns out to be closer to the truth than that put forward by the 'expert', who has received extensive instruction in the subject.

It is not practical for me to keep stating that I may be wrong. Also, there is insufficient space to delve into the many academic arguments as to why a particular option has been picked as having the highest chance of being correct. For those who want to go further into the subject there are Notes and References at the end of the book. They enlarge on some topics and point to some of the literature.

The views of those involved in Biblical studies vary greatly. When considering a work it is well to keep in mind the chances that even the most forthright declaration can be subject to error.

It is not easy to put a figure to these chances. An estimate, even if inaccurate, is useful since it gives a broad measure of the truth. When reading an academic work, or the work of an ancient author, I interpret definite statements —those which use terms such as 'was', or 'we know that'— as being correct only three times out of four.

Statements which have the slightest hint of uncertainty —which use terms such as 'likely' or 'probably'— could be correct in every other case.

When vague terms are used —such as 'might have', 'may be', or 'possibly'— I treat them as pure speculation.

The chances of statements in this book being right or wrong are no different.

The purpose of this book, based on the results of 20th century thought and research, is to explain the event sequence of the ministry of Jesus as portrayed in John's gospel. In order to do this it is necessary to set it within the framework in which John was writing. It is then that the teaching of Jesus can be fully appreciated.

The book is in two parts.

The first part 'Setting the Scene' includes background material taking the reader on a journey to the Fourth Gospel.

The second part 'The Story of Jesus as told by John' draws on the other gospels using them to fill out the Johannine events. The ideas put forward by John A .T. Robinson in his book *The Priority of John* published posthumously (SCM: 1985) have been used extensively. Not all scholars accept his arguments but much makes sense to me.

It is strange how few church members have a grasp of the event sequence of Jesus' ministry as depicted by John. It is not taken seriously maybe because Religious Education in our schools neglects the subject preferring to rely on the other simpler gospels.

This book is not a companion to the New Testament to use whilst studying different Bible passages, nor is it a discussion about Jesus' teaching; there are plenty of works in those fields. Suggestions are not made as to what you should believe.

I hope that, as a result of reading this book, you will find studying the Bible as stimulating and rewarding as I have.

BACKGROUND INFORMATION

Background information is given throughout the text in boxed areas. These boxes do not form part of the writing, and they can be ignored whilst reading the main composition if the reader finds them intrusive.

Supplementary information is given at the end under Notes and References. Once again, the notes are not intended to be read at the same time as the main text. They are for use by those who wish to examine the subject in greater depth.

PART 1

SETTING THE SCENE

THE FIRST SUCCESSFUL POPULAR LIFE OF JESUS

Ernest Renan who was born in 1823 wrote a successful and popular *Life of Jesus*. He stated that in his opinion the historical story in the Fourth Gospel, the Gospel of John, is the Life of Jesus.

He also said that in writing the discourses —the long speeches of Jesus recorded in the gospel— John introduced a new mystical language which was not known in the other gospels. Examples of words used in a special way in this language were 'world', 'truth', 'life', 'light' and 'darkness'.

1 THE TWO ASPECTS OF GOD

Rainbows are marvellous. Like magic, they suddenly appear with soft colours delicately shining against a dark rainy background. The ends just seem to melt away, fading to nothing. Trying to spot where I would start to dig for the mythical pot of gold is a game that gives me much pleasure. The end moves as you move, and comes and goes as the rain and sun play over the landscape. You think you have an answer, then you haven't.

Trying to understand people is much the same. Moods and ideas change as time moves on and, like finding the rainbow's end, fully to understand another, or even ourselves, is impossible. At least we can start by just looking at the colours of other people's personalities which often delicately shine against dark rainy backgrounds.

But it is not easy as we are strange creatures. Some are prepared to kill others in the good name of religion. These passionate feelings about religion are often fuelled by the views or beliefs we think that others hold. Yet we seldom try to find out exactly how others see God, and what is behind their beliefs. For some reason it is not fashionable to discuss religion or even our own feelings about God; and we are the poorer for it.

Finding out how others think is like gaining physical fitness. If we want to keep in trim we exercise by playing games or walking in the countryside which can be fun as well as being good for us. To explore the views of others and try to understand what they are thinking are also fun. It is one way of helping us to keep spiritually fit, to keep our feet on the ground, and to enable us to stay in contact with God.

Talking about religion and how we feel about it is quite difficult. A hundred years or more ago, when religion was much more a topic of conversation, people were accustomed to using special religious words. But today, the range of words we use when we do talk about spiritual things is quite small.

A survey of our understanding of words used in the bible and hymns produced surprisingly poor results. To make matters more difficult, religious words used by different churches can have different meanings. A simple word like 'Sin' can be a pitfall.

Some Churches tell their members exactly which actions are sinful. In others, the word sin is defined very generally and can be taken to mean any action likely to harm your neighbour, or not being in contact with God. Even within one church people attach different meanings to words and may change them over the years. Misunderstandings are common, no wonder there are conflicts!

There is nothing new in people not understanding what others are trying to say, or not grasping why others have certain feelings. The Bible is full of such conflicts. Before going further and discovering what was behind those conflicts, we need to find some way to make it easier for ourselves to understand others. We need a way to help us get behind the words so that we can get nearer to the speaker or writer.

There is a method which can help us, and that is by realising that we use models to aid our thoughts. God is perceived in different ways, and by finding how others see God we can go some way to appreciating their point of view. The method is not foolproof since we are all so different, and our knowledge of God depends on our past experience. The way we think and how we view things is set by our background and childhood which vary from person to person.

To make sense of our surroundings and cope in the jungle of this world, we build models in our minds. We invent and make up what we don't know. We can see this in action when we travel from our home to another place some distance away. We build in our mind's eye a picture of its direction and its relation to other places, but when we look at a map we often find that we were miles out. The model may not be strictly accurate, and in most cases it does not matter since it helps us to get about. We cannot possibly know everything, so to help us along we guess and fill in the missing bits.

But we have to be very careful. We can be very wrong particularly when we build our pictures of other people. We often base our model on outward appearances, and it is not until we get to know a person properly that we find that we made a misjudgement. How many times have we wrongly thought someone was wonderful, or someone we were most suspicious of turned out to be a real friend?

To help us understand what someone is saying or thinking we need to appreciate the model they are using at that particular

10

time. There are two types of model or ways of thinking, one is connected with language and the other with feelings or intuition.

These two ways are based on the two sides of the brain. It is easy to oversimplify, but as a general guide we know that the two sides of the brain each contribute to our thinking in different ways, giving two complementary ways of knowing things. Roughly, as there is much overlap, the left side is the centre for intellectual, analytical and language thought; the right side for imaginative, intuitive and non-verbal thought.

	THE TWO SIDES OF THE BRAIN	
	RIGHT SIDE	LEFT SIDE
Characteristic	Intuitive Spatial perception	Intellectual Analytical
Examples	Music Crafts Imagination	Reading Writing Arithmetic

Understanding that there are two ways of thinking has given direct benefit to many people. Those who never thought that they were able to draw or paint have suddenly been able to do so by being taught to use the right, non-verbal side of the brain. Some art schools now use this method.

In broad terms we can also perceive God in two ways, and these two aspects of God are, in the end, the same.

Firstly, there is the language aspect or model, which is linked to the way we speak of things. This picture is of God as a father figure. He is wholly other and in control of both the cosmos and world. In an exaggerated case He is seen 'up there' in heaven and in total control as a sort of king managing the universe. Many of us use the word 'He' when speaking of this aspect of God as, by tradition, the idea of God as the strong male ruler has been handed down to us from the past. If one were bad one might be punished by a thunderbolt, and if good rewarded by good fortune and becoming prosperous.

Today, the images we have are not quite like that, but it does give an indication of what God in control means. I refer to this aspect of God as 'God the Father'.

11

In the second way or model, God is viewed as pure spirit and is seen as relationships within or without oneself. It is only an 'inward feeling' and has no picture which can be described in words. God is spirit outside the space and time which we are bound by, and is separate from, though interwoven with, the universe. This aspect of God is seen to operate in an indirect way working through the natural order of things.

If we act in a selfish way, such as over-exploiting the environment, then in due course 'nature' will see that we suffer for it. If we abuse our bodies when young by over- or under-eating, or using harmful drugs, we may damage our health later in life. We could say that this side of God is understood as part of our subconscious mind, always present yet not in a direct way.

Much of John's gospel seeks to portray God as such; double meanings, riddles, contradictions are used in an attempt to communicate what cannot be said in words. Images such as Light, The Word, Old Testament Wisdom, Spirit of Truth and Father are employed, many of which were probably used by Jesus. I call this way 'God the Spirit'.

There are many terms which could be used to describe the two aspects of God, but none gives an exact description. Many of the terms are interwoven between the two strands and not all the paired words are opposites. Here is a list:-

GOD the FATHER	GOD the SPIRIT
Cosmological	Ontological
────────	────────
Male, Creator	Female, Mother
God Loves	God is Love
Outside Me	Inside Me
Looks after Me	Part of Me
Transcendent	Immanent
Orthodox	Gnostic
Western	Eastern
Theistic	Mystical
Deistic	Naturalistic
Supranaturalistic	I Am
Conservative	Understand with Heart
Theological	Philosophical

Prayer in its various forms plays a large part in a religious person's life. When we come face to face with illness we become more aware of how prayer brings God closer and at the same time we appreciate better what this life is about. Perhaps those who have had a prayerful life can cope with illness and the prospect of death more easily.

The prayers which are said in church are mostly directed to the 'God the Father' aspect of God, asking for things or just giving thanks. Interestingly when a prayer is heard many times over, such as week after week in a church which uses prayers out of a book, the meaning behind the prayer can become embedded in us. The contents are understood without listening to the meaning of the words and, freed from this distraction, we are more aware of, and able to be moved by, the underlying poetry. The prayer is changed from the language type of prayer to the wordless type of the mystic, where the meaning comes out of oneself in what could be described as feeling or understanding.

When praying for others who need upholding or who are asking for healing, energy or love which we receive ourselves through prayer is out-poured toward that person. This prayerful energy is similar to the power Jesus felt going from him when the woman wishing to be healed touched his cloak.

> And straightway Jesus, perceiving in himself that the power from him had gone, turned him about in the crowd and said, 'Who touched my garments?' And his disciples said unto him, 'You see the multitude swarming around you, and yet you say "Who touched me?"'
>
> And he looked round about to see her that had done this thing. But the woman fearing and trembling, knowing what had happened to her, came and fell down before him, and told him all the truth. And he said to her, "Daughter, your faith has made you whole; go in peace, and be well of your affliction."   Mark 5:30-34

The importance of prayer is that we can make ourselves open to receive this loving power or grace. It is living our lives in the spirit.

The way God is perceived often cuts across churches, friends and families, and although like-minded people tend to come together there is normally a good mixture of different views in any one Church. Also, we may change our view depending on the circumstances at the time. In times of crisis, just before some event which frightens you —such as before an operation— God can appear like a real parent in our crying prayer 'God help me'.

But at other times, or perhaps later on in our life when

someone we love has died, we may come close to the mystery of the pure spiritual side of God.

One approach to God is not right and the other wrong, even if we happen to feel that one way is deeper and the other shallower. They are different, and depend on our culture and the way we have been taught in our childhood. Some people go strongly to one side, other people to the other side, but most of us have the potential for understanding both ways. Those who are exceptionally spiritual —the sort of person one occasionally meets who is obviously close to God, and simply shines with holiness— seem to accept both aspects as quite natural. That is what we should aim for.

Those with extreme views on a particular aspect will often argue their case with dogma and rigid beliefs. It is by looking at these beliefs and the arguments being put forward that we can get an understanding of the model or aspect of God they have in mind.

We must always remember that any model is but a pale representation of the real thing, just as the imaginary map we use to find our way around is not as accurate as an Ordnance Survey map. Even the blobs and green patches on that Ordnance Survey map itself give only a hint of the richness of life and colours seen when we journey past houses, woods, fields. So the way we perceive God is only a small part of the picture.

We are not concerned with particular Christian beliefs in this book. These are up to the reader to decide in the light of the message given by Jesus in the New Testament. But, by better communication and understanding of what other people think, we may ourselves move forward in our search.

This table summarises the types of belief held on various subjects by those who perceive God as 'God the Father' and those who perceive God as 'God the Spirit'. Most people quite naturally see both aspects and happily run the two side by side. One way is not better than the other, and in the end they are both the same. Extreme and oversimplified cases have been listed for clarity.

The left hand column shows the various subjects, and a brief summary of how each group feels about the subject is shown in the two right hand columns.

SUBJECT	GOD THE FATHER ASPECT	GOD THE SPIRIT ASPECT
VIEW OF WORLD	–Is good. –Our sinning is responsible for the bad in the world	–Is bad: e.g. famine, floods, cancer –The God in us spreads 'light' in the darkness of the world.
DEVIL AND EVIL	–Subservient to God. –Spiritual nature which tempts us.	–The same order as God as exampled by light and darkness.
VIEW OF JESUS	–Jesus is Lord and Son of God. –Sent to save us from sin and to redeem us. –Miraculous birth and life.	–Jesus and mankind receive their being from the same source. Jesus is divine through the Word, and he is our guide to our spiritual lives.
MIRACLES AND HEALING	–Demonstration of the power of God.	–Demonstration of faith and how things are.
PRAYER TYPE	–Supplication, intercession. –Is strong individually.	–Wordless exchange of 'energy'. –Is strong in group.

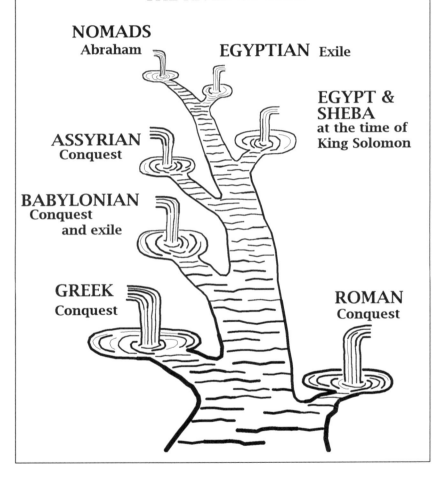

SOME INFLUENCES ON JEWISH CULTURE AT THE TIME OF JESUS

THE RIVER OF TIME

NOMADS
Abraham

EGYPTIAN Exile

EGYPT & SHEBA
at the time of
King Solomon

ASSYRIAN
Conquest

BABYLONIAN
Conquest
and exile

GREEK
Conquest

ROMAN
Conquest

2 CONFLICT: NOMADS AND SETTLERS

It is instructive to watch television programmes showing how other people live. It makes us realise that those things we take for granted can be completely foreign to people with other life styles. When I see pictures of the wandering nomads with their flocks of sheep and goats, I think of the Old Testament tribes which also lived a semi-nomadic life moving on to the next place when new pastures were needed. It was, and is, a hard way of life, but many people who live like this, both then and now, would not change. Being so close to nature for them is far better than the rush of city life.

We who live in our comfortable houses perhaps get an inkling of what it feels like during holidays when we go camping and 'get back to nature'. Without the pressures of books, newspapers and possessions we come much closer to that wordless nature of God.

In much the same way, the wandering tribes in Old Testament times saw this aspect of God in action; in the weather, in how the flocks of animals behaved, and in how they themselves were provided for. The woods, the grassy pastures and water belonged to everyone as it was all part of nature or God. God and nature are, in some ways, the same thing. They felt that they were part of it all —as we say today— a part of the wholeness of the physical and spiritual creation. Those who tried to alter this natural order of things, such as the settled farmers and city-dwellers, were seen as going against God.

Not only were the people who lived in villages and towns seen to be interfering with nature by planting crops, but they also took the best land and allowed no one else to come on it. This they could do because of their superior technology. Being settled they could manufacture good quality equipment, swords and armour, and build defences which made surprise attacks against them difficult.

Today we can see the same process with some primitive tribes living in the tropical forests. They hold no property, they see the forest as providing a living for all, and they are slowly being squeezed out of their traditional way of life.

The Old Testament contains many stories of the battles

between the settlers and the nomads or semi-nomads. The story of Cain and Abel in Genesis 4:1-16 is an example of these struggles. It could be a very ancient tale being handed down from generation to generation.

Abel was the nomad keeping animals and Cain was the settler farmer. Both brought offerings to God. Abel's offering was acceptable but Cain's offering of his harvest was not. Cain the farmer killed Abel the nomad, and God condemned the murder. The story goes on to say that if anyone tried to harm Cain in return, they would suffer seven times as much. Although right is seen to be on the side of Abel the nomad it is Cain the settler city dweller who comes off best because of his superior technology.

These tensions between the two ways and attitudes to God can be traced all the way through both the Old and New Testaments. The logical thinking and successful 'doers' like the settlers on the one hand, and on the other hand the poorer, perhaps less well-educated people such as the nomads, who are very close to God but in a different way.

As time went on two major changes took place. The wild wooded countryside started to disappear as most of the nomads became settlers, but the tension between the two ways continued although in a different form.

All the pictures we see today of the Holy Land and the surrounding countries are of desert scrubland with irrigated fields growing crops. It is not easy for us to imagine how different it must have been four thousand years ago when Abraham led his tribe through the land. Why was he able to do this without too much opposition from the people already living there? At that time the fertile valleys were producing figs, fruit, barley, wheat, cattle and were even exporting oil and wine to Egypt as well as the long straight cedar-wood tree trunks from Lebanon. The local people would have been numerous and strong.

He was able to travel through the land because the hills and mountains were wooded. It was the valleys and places with streams and shallow water-holes, able to supply animals and crops during the dry seasons, which had been cleared of trees first, and where the majority of people lived. But the hill country, where water was not so easy to find, was covered with uncleared forests.

The Book of Genesis tells us that Abraham was living a semi-nomadic life in these very places. His tribe with their cattle were able to survive because they had the technology to dig deep wells. Most of these where were dug were on the watershed, the crest of the highland ridge where water drains down on either side of the hill, and where there are few springs. Indeed Abraham's grandson Jacob dug a well at Sychar, the well where Jesus talked to the woman of Samaria in chapter 4 of John's gospel.

As the land was fought over the woods were either burnt or cut down to make defences until, at the time of Jesus, there must have been only patches left.

Later, during the great revolt when the Romans in AD 70 were attacking Jerusalem and had it under siege, the Jewish historian Josephus wrote:

> And now the Romans, although they were finding great difficulty in getting materials, raised their platforms in twenty-one days having cut down all the trees that were in the countryside around the city for a distance of about ten miles.
>
> And truly, the very view itself of the country was a melancholy thing; for those places which were before adorned with trees and pleasant gardens were now become a desolate country in every way, and its trees were all cut down.
>
> Josephus, Jewish War

During this time the population in Palestine was probably quite large at about three million, perhaps not much less than today. A very different place since the days when Abraham led his small band tending its flocks through the country.

The countryside had changed completely because the increased population chopped down trees and planted crops, but what did not change so easily were the traditions and ideas of the people. You only have to think of how some groups living today have not altered their ways for hundreds of years. The Romany Gypsies first recorded in Europe in 1417 probably came from India many years before that. Their way of life, preferring to travel and live in caravans, has changed little despite persecution over the centuries. Likewise the nomadic tradition lived on with the tensions and misunderstandings continuing.

The circumstances had changed in that the wandering tribes had become settlers themselves, but they still felt that they were the ones God had chosen. As descendants of Abraham they were

19

Jews and believed in the one God. The other settlers were Gentiles, or those who are not Jews.

Over the years it was the Jews that became the leaders of the country, having taken over from the original peoples, and they were the ones who were in control as landowners. As you would expect, now that their lifestyle had changed living in comfort with servants, many were not 'walking with God', in the old way. It was the Prophets who kept having to recall them to return to the true God.

The prophet Amos lived at a time very much like ours, with growing prosperity which was not reaching everybody, and that was 850 years before Jesus. The wealthy had become corrupt and the poor who worked the land were no better off. He was saying:

They hate him that stands up for justice in court,
and they detest him that speaketh uprightly.

Because you trample upon the poor,
and extract from them wheat:–

you have built houses of hewn stone, but shall not dwell in them;
you have planted pleasant vineyards, but you shall not drink the wine.

For I know how many are your wrongdoings
and how mighty are your sins;
you that afflict the just, that take a bribe,
and turn aside the needy in the courts from obtaining justice,
which is their right.

Therefore he that is prudent shall keep silence in such a time;
for it is an evil time.

Seek good, and not evil, that you may live:
and so the Lord, the God of hosts, shall be with you, as you say.

Hate the evil, and love the good,
and establish judgement in the courts;
then it may be that the Lord, the God of hosts,
will be gracious unto you.

Amos 5:10-15

It was the poor who worked the land who were often the ones close to God in the nomad tradition. They were at times referred to as the *'am ha-aretz* meaning 'people of the land'. In their struggle for survival they were unschooled and unable to study

20

the Bible texts. As a result, to the educated and better off they seemed to be lacking in godliness. But many of the prophets came from this nomadic background, and they saw their job as reminding the nation that the relationship with God was all important.

TWO WRITERS

Useful sources of information about the Jews comes from two writers, Josephus and Philo of Alexandria. It is from Josephus that we have gained much knowledge of the events and history around the time of Jesus.

Flavius Josephus

Was born AD 37 and died sometime after AD 100. He was a priest and a scholar. He spent a couple of years in Rome just before the Jewish revolt which started in AD 66. At the start of the war he was appointed one of the leaders in Galilee, but he was captured. He joined the Roman side obtaining favour with the Roman commander by prophesying that he, the Roman commander Vespasian, would one day become emperor. He then lived in Rome and wrote four books:-

1. 'Bellum Judaicum', *Jewish War* dated about AD 75.
   Account of the Jewish war with a Roman bias.

2. 'Antiquitates Judaicae', *Jewish History* dated about AD 93.
   Jewish history from the time of the Exile.

3. 'Vita', *Life* written sometime after AD 95.
   An account of his life.

4. 'In' or 'Contra Apionem', *Against Apion* written later than AD 97.
   Apion was an anti-Jewish writer and this work puts the
   other side of the argument.

Philo of Alexandria

Lived at Alexandria in Egypt and died AD 40. He wrote about Jewish law and theology mainly for Gentile readers. There was a strong Jewish presence in Egypt and even another Jewish temple.

21

THE PENTATEUCH: THE FIRST FIVE
BOOKS OF THE OLD TESTAMENT
How the writings of many people were brought together.

When King Solomon died in 922 BC his kingdom broke into two, Judah in the south and Israel in the north.

In Judah in the south the stories and traditions were put into writing. They showed Aaron, the brother of Moses, in a very favourable light, maybe because the priests were descended from Aaron. They referred to God as 'Yahweh' (which in German is written with a J) —or 'Jehovah'— and so scholars called these texts 'J'.

In Israel, the northern kingdom, the stories and traditions were also put into writing. They concentrate on Moses, and his brother Aaron is shown less favourably. The word used for God was 'Elohim' and, as a result, scholars could trace which texts were connected. They called these passages 'E' standing for Elohim.

Israel in the north was conquered by the Assyrians in 722 BC and many fled to the south.

To unite those who fled from Israel in the north with the people of the South the two texts were put together and interwoven into one. As the texts were considered 'holy' neither could be deleted so that many stories are repeated with different accounts of the same incident. This is 'JE'.

Both 'E' and 'J' portrayed God as a person, who talks to people and walks on the earth, very much the 'God the Father' aspect of God we discussed in chapter one.

The Priests of the time wrote down rules which they and the people should follow. These included the need to worship and sacrifice only at the temple. Because they were written by priests these writings are known as 'P'. Probably written during the reign of King Hezekiah who died in 687 BC.

They saw the 'God the Spirit' aspect of God and to counter some of the 'God the Father' in 'JE' they rewrote the stories as they saw them.

During the reign of King Josiah 'D' was written, mostly about the history of the Jewish people, mainly in the book of Deuteronomy. Some scholars suggest that a second edition was written after the conquest of Judah and exile to Bablyon in 587 BC.

Later still someone else put together all the sections into an historical order, with further bits added to help join the sections. The result is a wonderful mixture of all the aspects of God. For instance, the 'God the Father' aspect of God in 'JE' is seen when God is thought of as a person and forgives people their sins —is merciful— or punishes, whilst in the 'God the Spirit' 'P' writings one gets what one deserves in the natural order of things.

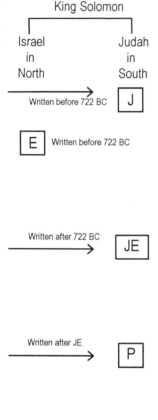

King Solomon

Israel in North — Judah in South

Written before 722 BC — J

E — Written before 722 BC

Written after 722 BC — JE

Written after JE — P

Written about 622 BC
2nd edition after 587 BC — D

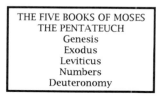

THE FIVE BOOKS OF MOSES
THE PENTATEUCH
Genesis
Exodus
Leviticus
Numbers
Deuteronomy

3 THE JEWISH WAY

What is the connection between a doctor, a nurse, a potter, a silversmith, a cleaner, someone who makes cheese, a shepherd, a judge, a king and a mother or father? Answer: they are just some of the rich and different images of God used in the Old Testament. The wonderful diversity of writings in both the New and Old Testaments arises from the fact that many people had a hand in writing and editing the texts. So the Bible is not a single book, it is much more a library of different writings.

The Old Testament writings are very ancient and there is a considerable amount of duplication where two versions of the same story have been included. For example, there are two accounts of how the world was created, and two lists of the ten commandments. The two accounts are not always completely separate in different parts but are sometimes mixed up together in the same chapter as in the case of the story of the flood.

We saw in the last chapter how the nomads and the settlers were in conflict over ideas about God, and how with time they came together. It was the same with the writings. Some of this duplicated material is told from the side of the settlers and other sections are told from the side of the nomads and those who followed in that tradition. Then, broadly speaking, these two strands were woven together when the first part of the Old Testament was put into writing probably 800 years before Jesus. See opposite for an explanation on how some scholars think it evolved.

You would think that putting different views of the nature of God together into one set of holy writings would cause disagreements. Those who believed one thing would object to the others views. It was not like that in those days because what you believed was not as important as keeping God's laws.

We often find it difficult to understand that beliefs cannot be important to religion because our Western Christianity is built around beliefs. We live with the fact that many churches do not consider you to be a true 'Christian' unless you share their particular set of beliefs, such as about Jesus, baptism or sin. The Jews, throughout the period including in New Testament times, did not think you were less of a Jew if your theology was different from someone else's. The Sadducees did not believe in the afterlife, whilst the Pharisees did, but they all saw themselves as fully Jewish, even if they did argue about it.

It was how well you kept God's laws that mattered, and these laws were set out in the Torah, meaning 'Teaching' or 'The Law'. In effect the Torah is set out in the first five books of the Old Testament —known as the Pentateuch or the Five Books of Moses— and, for the individual, the ten commandments were, and still are for Jews, the central part.

THE THREE JEWISH TEMPLES

1. King Solomon (who died in 922 BC) built the first temple to replace the 'Tent of the Presence' where God was thought to reside and was worshipped. It was destroyed in 586 BC.

2. Not long after the first temple was destroyed, a second temple was built by the exiles who returned from Babylon. It was a copy of the first temple but simpler and was dedicated on the Passover feast in 516 BC.

3. King Herod in 20 BC enlarged and rebuilt the second temple and the surrounding area on a grand scale in white stone. It was this third temple that Jesus visited, and it was destroyed by the Romans in AD 70.

The greatest part of the law consists of rules of conduct connected with the temple sacrifices and purity. As God was seen to have a presence in the temple the priests and others had to approach the holy place in a clean and pure condition. Rather like putting on your Sunday best to go to church or dark clothing to a funeral out of respect. If a sacrifice had to be made the priest making it had to be in a state of purity.

The purity rules did not greatly affect the ordinary person except on special days and feasts, but it was the priests that officiated in the temple that were the ones that had to mind the purity laws. The story of the Good Samaritan told in Luke 10 is about the Priest and Levite and the purity laws.

PRIESTS AND LEVITES

The priests were directly descended from Aaron but the Levites, who worked with the priests and probably also obeyed the purity rules, were not. They were descended from Aaron's father Levi.

Had the man lying beside the road been dead then the pries touching the body would have become impure. Corpse-impurity for a priest was strictly banned, the only exception being if he had contact with the corpse of an extremely close relative living in the same house. These and other rules are set out in Leviticus. So the priest was not just funking attending to a wounded person. He had responsibilities not to get involved so that he could carry out his duties in the temple. The question raised by the story is how far should society be governed by rules which do not give priority to people.

The purity laws were not designed for everybody to be in a state of purity the whole time. Nor did they suggest that anyone not in a state of purity was bad. They were telling how Jews, and particularly the priests, were to achieve purity and keep purity when the need occurred. Getting into a state of purity was often not difficult as it was simply a matter of ritual prayer at sundown.

THE MAIN RELIGIOUS PARTIES

The three main Jewish religious parties in New Testament times were:

1. Sadducees: The priests who ran the temple in Jerusalem were mainly Sadducees. They had a great deal of power and ran the country under the Romans. They obeyed the laws as set down by Moses, and they did not believe in an afterlife.

2. Pharisees: They lived strict lives obeying the laws as set out by Moses. As well as the laws of Moses they added the interpretations which were handed down over the years. They believed in an afterlife, which had a strong appeal to the ordinary person.

3. Essenes: A group who split themselves off from other Jews because they did not accept the priests who ran the temple, and considered that they were the rightful priests of the temple. Some Essenes lived as monks totally separate from other Jews, and others lived in communities of both men and women. They all lived to very strict rules laid down by their group which attempted to follow the law in all its exactness.

After the Jewish war ended in AD 72 only the Pharisees remained as an effective group. They were caring and considerate and not all bad as portrayed in the gospels.

It was the Scribes who interpreted the law. Originally they just read and wrote for others, but in time they became much more than that. They were the 'legal experts'. As lawyers today, you get different answers according to how you looked at a matter. The Scribes were not a religious party, although no doubt individually they belonged to different groupings.

There were three major religious parties before the revolt of AD 66 and the subsequent destruction of Jerusalem by the Romans.

Within the groups and without there were a number of different beliefs and shades of opinions, although, as we have said, all saw themselves very much as one people with the one God and sacrifices at the temple. Like today, people could change from one group to another. Josephus, the Jewish historian, tells us that he was able to join each of the main religious parties in turn; this is what he says:

> "And when I was about sixteen years old, I wanted to try out the several sects that were among us. These sects are three:- the first is that of the Pharisees, the second that of the Sadducees, and the third that of the Essenes, as I have frequently told you; for I thought that by this means I might choose the best, if I were once acquainted with them all; so I contented myself with hard fare, and underwent great difficulties, and went through them all."
>
> Josephus, Jewish War

In the end he emerged as a Pharisee.

SACRIFICES IN THE TEMPLE

Sacrifices were made, not to gain favour with God, but to help the person making the sacrifice to come closer to God. Giving away something of value is a way of disciplining oneself. In today's terms it is like giving up luxuries during Lent, or perhaps going without food for a few days to help one's spiritual development. If someone had become ritually unclean, an offering or sacrifice to put them back into a state of holiness had to be made. Sacrifices could not be used to put right a non-religious sin, such as stealing.

Sacrifices or offerings are detailed in the Old Testament in Leviticus chapters 1 to 7. Animals, vegetables and drink were offered. An animal, such as a bullock, a sheep, goat or dove, was killed and, depending on the type of sacrifice, it was burnt or part of it was burnt. In some cases the meat from the animal was given to the priests. The animal had to be in good condition, so it was no good getting rid of the shabbiest and oldest goat in your flock, it had to be the best! In Jerusalem, on the site of where the temple was, there is a 'basement' cut out of the rock to hold the blood from the sacrifices. To us today it would have been very unpleasant.

The prophets of old, as well as Jesus, were often telling the people that it is the inward attitude to worship that mattered. Just because you had made a sacrifice did not put everything to rights. The prophet Amos pronounced on those who did not live up to their words and were unredeemable sinners.

> Thus saith the Lord:-
>   I hate, I despise your feasts;
>   and I will take no delight in your solemn assemblies.
>   Though you offer me your burnt and other offerings,
>   I will not accept them:
>   neither will I look upon the peace offerings of your fat beasts.
>   Amos 5:21-22

27

THE THREE JEWISH PILGRIM FEASTS

Before it was destroyed in AD 70 the temple was the centre for sacrifices and religious ceremonies. Exodus 34:22-23 declares that all males are to appear before the Lord at the temple three times a year at the feasts of Passover, Pentecost and Tabernacles. Pilgrims came to Jerusalem in thousands for these feasts, but it was only the wealthy or those who lived nearby who would be able to go regularly. For those living abroad the pilgrimage could have been a once in a lifetime event.

Passover Feast and time of Unleavened Bread (In Hebrew *Pesach*).

The Passover and time of Unleavened Bread were originally separate celebrations which then came together into one. There is a description of the event in the Old Testament (Deuteronomy 16:1-8). The festival itself lasted a week with time being spent getting ready the day beforehand. As the Jewish day started at sundown in the evening, and the feast started then, the day beforehand was in effect the day the feast started as we understand it. So it was during that afternoon that the lambs which were going to be eaten at the Passover meal were taken to the temple to be killed by the priests. Blood from the lambs was sprinkled on the altar as an offering. The lamb was then taken to a home in the city of Jerusalem to be roasted and eaten after sunset.

The meal was to remember God's deliverance at the time when Moses led the Jews away from being slaves in Egypt. During the whole week only unleavened bread, bread which had not been made light and fluffy by fermentation using yeast, was to be used.

Note that the festival had to involve the temple for the killing of the lambs and that the meal was be to eaten in Jerusalem. With so many pilgrims coming to the city it could be a time of tension with riots started by agitators so the Roman occupying force was put on stand by.

Festival of Pentecost, Weeks, Harvest or Day of Firstfruits (*Shavuot*).

This was a one day harvest festival which took place after a 'week of weeks' (7 weeks which is 49 days) from the time of the Passover festival. Deuteronomy 26:1-11 tells of baskets of the first part of the crops being brought to the temple. In Acts 2:1 we read that the followers of Jesus were together at this feast when they received the Holy Spirit.

Festival of Tabernacles (*Sukkot*).

Huts were constructed using branches for the week long festival. The people slept and ate in the shelters to commemorate the wandering in the wilderness. The ceremonies included lighting large candles in the temple.

4 THE FREEDOM MOVEMENT

By looking at the festivals of a nation we can gather an insight into the local culture, and can get a glimpse of the things which are important to the people. We have Christmas which, in England and Wales, has lost much of its time for religious reflection and has turned into an orgy of advertising, buying and eating, although on the positive side people's generosity can be seen in the presents we give and Christmas cards we send.

When reading the New Testament we feel the importance the festivals had for the population, and the theme which comes out is the struggle for freedom. We read of the week-long Passover festival commemorating the escape from bondage in Egypt, and other festivals including the feast of Tabernacles celebrating the newly won freedom of wandering in the wilderness following the enslavement in Egypt. Then there was the Feast of Lights remembering the time when the temple was rededicated in 164 BC after the successful Maccabees revolt. The three Jewish pilgrim feasts are set out on the opposite page, and two other important feasts are shown below.

TWO OTHER FEASTS

Dedication (*Hannukah*) or Feast of Lights.

The feast was to remember when the second temple was purified so that it could be used once again for Jewish worship. Originally it was polluted and stripped of its treasures by the occupying King, Antiochus Epiphanes. Then, following the successful revolt, Judas Maccabeus in 164 BC restored the temple and re-lit the sacred lamps (1 Maccabees 4:36-59) During the eight day feast Jerusalem would have been a blaze of lights.

Day of Atonement (*Yom Kippur*), The Fast (Acts 27:9) or High Sabbath.

A day of penitence and fasting. It was the only time that the High Priest was allowed to enter the Holy of Holies in the temple.

It was the inspiration of this successful revolt by the Maccabees which kept the threat of rebellion on the boil, and it was dangerous. Both Jesus and the people well knew of the massacres and misery which could be brought about by any rising against the Roman occupying forces. The horrors and excitement of the revolt are told in The First Book of the Maccabees, which for Protestant bibles is found in the Apocrypha.

THE APOCRYPHA

Parts of the Old Testament which are included in Roman Catholic bibles are left out of Protestant bibles and are part of a separate book, the Apocrypha. In broad, greatly simplified terms, these writings were not part of the ancient Jewish traditional Old Testament written in Hebrew.

Around 250 BC when the Hebrew scripts were first translated into Greek (The Septuagint Bible) these other writings were also translated and included with the traditional material.

This Greek bible was later translated into Latin (The Vulgate Bible) which was, and still is, the basis of the bibles used by the Roman Catholic church.

Later still, when the Protestants translated the Latin Bible into everyday language, they went back to the original Hebrew Bible. This meant leaving out the other writings included in the Greek Bible, the longer bits which went into the Apocrypha.

We need to look at what happened at the time of the Maccabees, even though it was nearly 200 years before Jesus' ministry, in order that it can help us understand why some saw Jesus as a military leader. It is also an exciting story.

In 167 BC the Jews had been under some form of continuous occupation or exile for five hundred years. At that time they were being ruled and exploited by the Syrian-Greek empire from the North, and the foreign ruling King, Antiochus Epiphanes, attempted to destroy Judaism and to convert the Jews away from their religion to the worship of the Olympian Zeus. So he stripped the Jewish temple in Jerusalem of all its treasures and ruthlessly tortured and killed men, women and children who showed the slightest opposition. As a result he was bitterly resented by all and particularly by those who lived in the countryside.

In an attempt to convert the population the King forced the Jewish leaders to make public sacrifices to the Greek God Zeus. But it had the opposite effect. In a village near Jerusalem, a priest, Mattathias Hasmoneas, was so angry at the betrayal by the Jewish leaders that he killed a fellow Jew who was making the sacrifice. Not only that, he did something seen to be much worse: he killed the Syrian official who was sent to check that the King's orders were being carried out.

Mattathias, together with his sons, fled into the wooded

hillsides and formed a guerrilla fighting force. Mattathias was clever and passed the leadership over to his third son Judas Maccabeus (The Hammer of the Heathens) who was a brilliant general. The band of guerrillas had the support of the villagers and rapidly grew in size. It was remarkable what happened.

Judas ambushed and raided the Syrians and was able to cut the supply lines to Jerusalem. At every victory he captured arms and recruited and trained a larger army. He defeated successions of invading forces, each larger than the last, which were sent from the north to annihilate him. The temple was purified and rededicated, and eventually after 25 years, by skilfully playing off the various opponents one against the other, the Jewish nation got complete independence.

Independence was, however, only for a short period. Further unrest occurred, and the Romans were invited in as allies. Their presence became an occupation but, because they had received help from the Jews in various battles, and because of the success of the past revolts, the Romans allowed the Jews to keep their own laws and customs. The occupation continued until a major revolt finally started in AD 66 (33 years after Jesus) and the Roman legions crushed all opposition. It caused the Dead Sea Scrolls to be hidden, The Essenes at Qumran to be obliterated, and the temple with its animal sacrifices to be utterly destroyed. The state of Israel was not re-established until modern times.

What do we know about the freedom movement and who were the Zealots which are often mentioned in books about the New Testament? All our information comes from the Bible and writers such as Josephus, and it is not easy to unravel the nuances and exact meanings of words which were used two thousand years ago.

The activities of the Jewish freedom movement and the people involved were labelled in many ways including Zealot, Sicarii, robber, and bandit as well as Pharisee and even Galilaean. To understand which group was being referred to is difficult particularly as at the time it was the custom not to name directly those being criticised. 'The Pharisees' in the gospels could be referring to the extreme Zealot movement rather than to the Pharisees in general.

The central theme of Judaism has always been that there is only one God. In the past Jews were able to live in an uneasy peace under the rule of eastern monarchs, such as the Babylonians. These monarchs owned the state and everything in it and had absolute power. For the Roman emperors it was different. Here the state had a life of its own including a Senate. To consolidate their power a number of emperors projected themselves as a God which was totally unacceptable to the Jews. The whole Roman machine under the emperor could be seen as paganism and anybody who, or any action that co-operated with the occupation forces was likewise directly opposing God. Paying taxes to the emperor was the same as recognising his divinity.

The name 'Zealot' was only given to those in the freedom movement by Josephus from the outbreak of the Jewish war. Nevertheless the word 'Zealot' has come to describe the freedom movement from the time of Herod the Great. It was not so much a formal sect, like the Essenes, but more of a coming together of Jews who had similar views. Like the Maccabees they had a great enthusiasm for God and the law; and were not nationalists or political freedom fighters, but were religious fanatics. In today's terms they were like some of the extreme religious groups who are prepared to kill and murder for what they see as God's cause. So revolt and murder was for them part of a holy war.

It is thought that the movement which was present during the lifetime of Jesus sprang from the extreme wing of Pharisaism, and may have first come together at the time of the census in AD 6/7. The listing of people and land for taxation purposes was seen as an acceptance that the country belonged to the Roman emperor rather than to God. As a result a revolt started which was led by Judas the Galilaean (mentioned in Acts 5:37) —who was probably the grandfather of the leaders of the Zealot fighters during the Jewish war.

Although Judas the Galilaean was killed, a well organised underground movement continued under a series of leaders. These fanatical Jews resolutely believed that the new age, the second creation, the rule of God, or kingdom where Israel would be supreme, would come if they worked with God to destroy the forces opposing God's will. For them there was no 'render unto Caesar' even those things belonging to Caesar. The question put to Jesus 'Is it lawful to pay taxes to Caesar?' may have been a test to see if Jesus was one of these die-hard Zealots.

Just before the Jewish war religious fanaticism reached such a

32

pitch that the Zealots resorted to numerous murders to further their aims. Any Jew who was opposed to an uprising against the occupying Roman forces was thought to be opposing God's plan, and was liable to be assassinated. Josephus, who was most critical of them, called them 'Sicarii', from the Latin word for a dagger which they used to terrorise the population. They hid these daggers in the folds of their clothes and would strike at any time.

The Sicarii were probably from the country districts where fanaticism was strong, but were active in Jerusalem and even in the temple area taking cover after their dirty deeds amongst the milling pilgrims. It is extremely unlikely that Judas Iscariot was a Sicarii, and the few scholars who have tried to make a connection between the names are far from convincing.

Jesus and his disciples, and later the early church members, were just as zealous. But they, in company with the Pharisees, knew that they could not force God to intervene in the world's affairs by starting a war with the 'ungodly' Roman occupying force. The second creation, the Kingdom of God had already started and was here if one only accepted it. No wonder the extremist Zealot Jews felt threatened by the doctrine of the gospels. It was these few fanatics who could have been behind the strong opposition to Paul and the early church. Jesus' followers would be seen as diluting the purity of Israel and postponing the day when God would rule the world.

When reading the New Testament and hearing the message of Jesus, it is not necessary to know exactly what each of the different groups and religious parties thought and we can leave the experts to debate their latest theories without losing anything. But we do need to understand some of the basic ideas or concepts which people held. Fortunately the Dead Sea Scrolls, which were discovered by chance in 1947, have given us a good insight into what one group, the Essenes, was thinking at that time. They also tell us that the graphic description which Josephus gives of the Essenes is not an exaggeration, although we must always remember that in some ways our understanding could be wrong.

Looking at the life and customs of the Essenes will give us an indication of the ideas held, even though Essenes were not numerous and had separated themselves from everyday life.

DEAD SEA SCROLLS

In 1947 the first of the Dead Sea Scrolls came to light in a cave overlooking the Dead Sea at Qumran where the Essenes lived. From eleven caves thousands of bits and pieces were found, some whole works, others just fragments. The scrolls were hidden in AD 68 just before Qumran was destroyed by the Roman legions when they were crushing the great rebellion. Two years later they sacked Jerusalem and obliterated the temple.

The scrolls could have been written by a number of different people rather than just the Essenes at Qumran.

They are important to us because:-

1. They tell us about the life and beliefs of the Jews at that time. For example we find that the range of different beliefs was greater than previously thought.

2. We now have evidence for the Old Testament about 1,000 years earlier than hitherto. Only a few small changes to the text had been made during this 1,000 year period. For example:

> A voice cried, "In the wilderness make..."

rather than   A voice in the wilderness cried "Make..."   (Isaiah 40:3)

3. Josephus (born AD 37) was an Essene for a trial period. His account of the sect is in line with the scrolls, and we now know that what he said was not a gross exaggeration.

The scrolls were made from animal hides which were treated and sewn together into a long strip. Lines were carefully ruled onto each panel to guide the writing. The ink was made from carbon and, as the writings were considered to be very holy no mistakes could be tolerated. For storage the scrolls were wrapped in linen cloth and put into jars.

5 THE ESSENE COMMUNITY

The Dead Sea lies in the rift valley 1,200 feet below sea level. The surrounding countryside is hot and dry, and the rugged brown mountains with their ravines and boulders make travel difficult. Even today much of the area is a desolate wilderness, except where the river Jordan winds its way down the valley from the north irrigating the green fields on either side. Near to where the river empties into the Dead Sea, on a high crag overlooking the sea, stands the ruins of a fortified monastery. In a cave within sight of the monastery, the first of the Dead Sea scrolls was discovered.

The monastery is at Qumran and, before the scrolls were found, the site was thought to have been just a hill fort.

Excavation and archaeological research showed that it was more than that, and it could have been the headquarters of the Essenes who copied and wrote many of the scrolls. If you visit the site you can see the remains of the rooms where the monks lived. There is an assembly room, a kitchen, a storeroom, and a writing room. Before eating the monks washed as a ritual, and there are at least two places for this ritual bathing. As rainfall is minimal water was stored in six large tanks cut into the rock.

The monastery was in an ideal place for monks who wanted to withdraw from the world. Today it still gives a feeling of the power of God. It is remote and the view of the Dead Sea is magnificent yet austere. I am sure many mountains and places with panoramic views are considered holy because, when you look down from them, the earth seems so vast. By comparison our day-to-day worries pale into insignificance. The impact must have been greater without the added benefit of flying and aerial photography, which we now take so much for granted.

Who were the Essenes? Translated the word means 'Pious Ones' and was the name for them that came into use by the general population, although they did not use it themselves. They were a very strict religious sect which separated itself from the mainstream of Jewish life.

The scrolls are not our only source of information about the Essenes. As we have seen, Josephus joined the Essenes for a time and wrote about them. Another Jewish writer, who was living at the time of Jesus, Philo of Alexandria, also wrote about them. Although we have these historical descriptions —as well as the Qumran scrolls— we cannot be sure that we have understood them correctly. The different accounts are not always absolutely clear, and the situation in the dim past was probably more complex than we think.

WHAT ARE THE DEAD SEA SCROLLS ABOUT?

Copies of all the Old Testament books were found except for one, the book of Esther. The more popular Old Testament books must have been in demand as more than one copy has been uncovered. There were also rule books for the Essene community telling them how they should live and they make fascinating reading.

In this summary of the scroll contents the international reference code for each scroll is shown in brackets. The first figure indicates where the first copy was found —the cave number and 'Q' for Qumran— followed by a code describing the writing. The document 'CD' was first found in Cairo.

For example:- (11Q Temple) shows that the writing was discovered in cave 11 at Qumran and is about the temple.

* *Old Testament:* All the books except Esther. No New Testament material.

* *Community Rule (1QS) or Manual of Discipline:* Handbook of instruction for the Essene leaders. Tells what the monks should, or should not, do.

* *Damascus Rule (CD):* Gives rules for the lay communities, rather than the monks, about such things as religious purity, diseases and marriage.

* *Messianic Rule (1QSa) or Rule of the Congregation:* How the world will be ruled and what will happen in the last days before the dawn of the new age. A short writing.

* *War Rule (1QM):* How a 40 year war leading up to the new age will be fought. All evil will be destroyed, including anyone not of the people of God, and in particular the Roman state. There will be a great spiritual battle between 'Sons of Light' and 'Sons of Darkness'.

* *Temple Scroll (11Q Temple):* Describes the new temple in the new age, the rituals and rules of behaviour. A long writing.

* *The Copper Scroll (3Q15):* Engraved on copper is a list of hidden treasures and where to find them.

* *Various:* Hymns, prayers and sayings.

* *Various:* Texts explaining the bible in different ways including stories.

* *Horoscopes (4Q186) & (4QMess ar):* The position of the planets at birth are related to how a person looks and their spiritual state. A forecast was made for a Messiah, or some important person maybe in the past.

The Essene community was organised rather like the collective farms and communes of today, where all money is held, and purchases made, by a treasurer. There was a strong sense of brotherhood, and possessions were held in common, even clothing. Josephus tells us that:

> Those that come to them must give what they have to be common to the whole order, so that among them all there is no appearance of poverty or excess of riches, but every one's possessions are intermingled with every other's possessions; and so there is, as it were, one means of support among all the brethren.
>
> Josephus, Jewish War

The brothers worked hard and in all weathers. In fields at the foot of Qumran, near the Dead Sea, they grew their food. Although everything else around was barren, just here there is a fresh water spring allowing palm trees to grow and cultivation to take place. They also made pots, cured hides and, of course, copied manuscripts.

Beside work, they regularly prayed at sunrise and sunset. The calendar they used was different from that used by the rest of the Jews and they followed carefully the different feast days as set out by their calendar. One third of each night was spent in prayer and study of the Torah and the interpretation of the Law. They saw themselves as keeping to the true Jewish way, as laid down by the Prophets. One of the scrolls, which they called the 'Community Rule', sets out the laws and rules they had to follow to achieve 'perfection'.

On joining the sect, the member had to take binding oaths. He had to obey every commandment of the law, keeping the secrets of the sect even under the worst torture. He had to observe justice towards all, hate the unjust, hold property in common, have humility, work hard and refuse to swear oaths or manufacture arms. The spiritual requirement of study, prayer and observance of the Jewish Sunday, the Sabbath, was also strict. But it was his spiritual state rather than the rituals that made him pure. The Community Rule says that when he is sprinkled with water he shall become clean by submitting his soul to everything God desires. To put it in a modern way, sprinkling with water will decontaminate him provided he has the correct attitude of mind to God.

Teaching was important and the rule goes on to say that the

master should educate all 'the sons of light', as they referred to themselves. Everyone was split into 'goodies' and 'baddies'; those who were 'born of truth' and 'come from a fountain of light' and those who were 'born of falsehood' and 'come from a source of darkness'. The good 'walk in the ways of light' and of course the wicked were governed by the 'Angel of Darkness'. It was the philosophy which fanatics have put forward for thousands of years in order to keep their members in line: 'If you do not think and do as I do, you are damned'.

```
        SOME ESSENE TASKS
 * Spent one third of a night in prayer
 * Prayed at sunrise & sunset
 * Ritually washed before eating
 * Ate in silence
 * Worked hard
 * Studied religious writings
 * Copied scrolls
 * Were expelled for breaking the law
     even in small ways
```

The total number at the Qumran monastery is estimated to have been no more than 150 to 200 men. Once a year all the monks met to be questioned on all matters concerning their spiritual progress and to be put into order of seniority. The newest recruit held the lowest position and at the top was the Leader or Guardian followed by the Treasurer and Priests. At any meeting with ten or more, whether it were for prayer or discussion, a priest had to be present.

The order was governed by a council headed by the Guardian. It consisted of three priests and twelve laymen who knew all the aspects of the Law. They would work with 'truth, uprightness, justice, compassion and humility'.

The twelve men symbolised the twelve tribes of Israel; and the three priests, the three clans of Levite priests. At the Council, anyone who wanted to speak had to ask permission of those present, and everyone had to be in their correct seating position depending on their importance. The priests first, the elders second, and then everyone else according to their position.

This rule probably also applied at meals which were important occasions. They ate in silence and only full members who were faultless in their observances of the rules could be present. The food or drink must not have been in any way contaminated during the meal or during cooking by, for instance, the use of 'unclean' pots and pans.

When and why did the Essenes go to Qumran? In the Scrolls there are many references to 'The Teacher of Righteousness' who set down the strict rules they followed. They held that he gave them the correct interpretation of the Law proclaimed by the Prophets. The scrolls do not tell us the name of 'The Teacher of Righteousness', but we do know that he lived at the time of the Maccabees. He was murdered and the scroll writings are full of sorrow and anger at his death. The murder may have been part of a power struggle for the temple leadership, perhaps by one of the Maccabean leaders after the revolt in 167 BC.

At that time most of the population actively supported Judas Maccabeus in the revolt against the Syrians. Later on, after the Jews had won the right to worship in their traditional way, things were different. Jonathan, the younger brother of Judas, became too powerful and ambitious. He accepted from the foreign Syrian King who was ruling at that time a post which many felt that he had no right to accept. He was made High Priest and religious leader in Jerusalem.

'The Teacher of Righteousness' and the group which were to become the Essenes could not tolerate the appointment which they saw as against the teaching of God. They therefore withdrew recognition of the temple worship, and had to retreat to the wilderness at Qumran.

ESSENES: THE VALID PRIESTS

The Essenes believed that the laws of the Bible did not allow the chief priests in Jerusalem to run the temple. It was their community at Qumran that were the real priesthood which should be organising the rituals for God. As priests they treated meal times as a holy or sacred occasion as if they were at the temple. Before eating they 'washed' by immersing themselves in large water cisterns. They then put on their white garments —the priests in Jerusalem wore white— and then took them off afterwards before going to work.

So far we have been considering the monks at Qumran but there were more Essenes than this, as Josephus tells us:

> They have no particular city but many of them dwell in every city; and if any of their sect arrives from other places, what is available is open for

39

their use just as if it were their own.

Josephus, Jewish War

So there must have been a network of monasteries or communities throughout the land, although Qumran was probably the headquarters. We are told that there were about 4000 in all —as against 6000 Pharisees. Some were monks, but there were others who lived ordinary lives earning their living in the normal way by trading and farming. They brought up children and employed servants, and lived together in small communes or groups both of men only, and of men and women. They kept themselves separate from others, only mixing for business.

The rules they had, as well as penalties for disobeying the rules, are listed in the Damascus Rule scroll. They are similar to those used by the monks but are tailored for everyday living. There is less emphasis on study but there are many restrictions on the Sabbath —the Jewish day of rest. There was to be absolutely no work of any kind as with Orthodox Jews today. They had to pay the equivalent of two day's wages a month into a fund to help their sick and poor.

```
ESSENES AND THE SABBATH
Some of the things lay members were NOT to do:-
        * BE NEAR TO GENTILES
        * SPEAK IDLE WORDS
        * MAKE DECISIONS ABOUT MONEY
        * MAKE LOANS
        * GO MORE THAN 500 YARDS
          AWAY FROM THE VICINITY
        * CARRY A CHILD
        * WEAR PERFUME
        * WEAR DIRTY CLOTHES
        * REPRIMAND A SERVANT
        * HELP THEIR ANIMALS
          e.g. at birth
```

Once a year they joined the Monks at Qumran to be questioned on all matters.

The Essene numbers were relatively small in relation to the population. All the same, their influence would have been considerable as they were widely distributed around the country. There must have been children who grew up and did not continue with the life, or others like Josephus who tried out membership of the sect and took some of the ideas with him. Although they kept themselves separate, there was an exchange of ideas and attitudes. Also, there may have been communities which were offshoots of the Essenes, living like them, but not subject to the discipline of Qumran.

What did the Essenes believe which caused them to live such lives? They thought that all evil in the world was shortly to end, and a new way of life would start. Haven't you ever thought how wonderful it would be if all the bad in the world was suddenly replaced by goodness? No quarrels, no wars, no sickness or unhappiness? For the Essenes God's Kingdom would be a Utopia, where only those living pure and godly lives would be accepted into a new and wonderful order, a return to the Garden of Eden.

The world would still be the same —the grass, the trees, and the animals— but it would be a perfect place. The animals would not attack each other and one would not suffer from the nasty side of nature such as stings and bites. Certainly there would be no soldiers occupying the land. Nobody expected to know exactly what the Kingdom would be like, but that did not matter, as it was all part of God's plan. But it would be everlasting. To quote from the Old Testament:

> The God of heaven shall set up a kingdom, which shall never be destroyed, nor shall the it's sovereignty be taken over by another people; but it shall break in pieces and consume all the kingdoms of these other people, and it shall stand for ever.
>
> Daniel 2:44

The Essenes thought that God had promised the new kingdom only to those who kept his commandments and laws as set out in the Old Testament. They saw themselves as the last people keeping these laws exactly as God wanted. It was because of them, because they had remained pure and godly in all the rituals, that the nation would survive and go into the new age.

What did they think would happen when the time came? We know from the Scrolls that they thought they would have to go into the desert, away from every contamination, so as to be ready to be used by God.

The Manual of Discipline, quoting from Isaiah 40:3, describes the scene by saying that the Essenes will detach themselves from living amongst 'bad men' and go into the wilderness 'to clear there the way of the Lord.'

There would be a massive cosmic battle of the good forces against the bad which would last for 40 years. It was somewhat like the space films we see today with the powers of evil being defeated by the few 'goodies' (mainly the Essenes themselves!) with right on their side. It would be a time of judgement when the bad would be destroyed.

How would they know when the end of the world was starting? They thought two things would happen:-

Firstly, a prophet would come forewarning that the time was at hand. People could then get ready for the final big battle. We do not know for sure, but it could be that they believed that the 'Teacher of Righteousness' was this final prophet. Other people were awaiting a second Elijah or someone equivalent. This prophet would announce that the battle was about to start and tell everybody whom God had chosen to lead them.

Secondly, the person chosen to lead them would take charge. This was the Messiah, and the word Messiah just meant 'the anointed one', like the kings in the past who were anointed. For most there would be only one Messiah, but the Essenes thought that there would be at least two. One would be a priest Messiah who would be the spiritual leader, directing the spiritual war, and be in overall command. The other would be a King Messiah fighting the battle on the ground, very much like the warrior kings of Israel in times past.

OLD TESTAMENT MESSIAH

The term 'Messiah' in Hebrew, or 'Christ' in Greek, originally was the word used for anyone whose position had been confirmed by anointing with holy oil. In the Old Testament it was mostly used to describe kings, and even describes the foreign Persian King Cyrus (Isaiah 45:1). Like most words the meaning changed over time. It came to refer to a future king who was expected to unite the Jews, throw out any occupying army and build a nation, as had King David in the past. The Messiah was mainly thought to be a warrior king who would fight and defeat all the enemies.

As we would expect, different people had different ideas as to what the Messiah would do and be like. It may have been only the

42

Essenes who thought that there would be two Messiahs. After two thousand years it is not easy for us to be clear as to what people were thinking. For instance, it may be that many ordinary people saw the occupying Roman soldiers as the major evil. In that case they might have thought that the Messiah was to be a warrior, a military king. They would expect him to lead them straight away into battle against the Romans, with God working miracles to help them to win.

There was an intense feeling throughout the country that the new age would be starting at any moment. Everybody was on the lookout for the Messiah, the man who would lead them toward that final hour of judgement. The place was abuzz with rumours that the Messiah had been seen, and that shortly they would be freed from oppression and want.

THE NEW TESTAMENT FALLS NATURALLY INTO FOUR PARTS

FIRST PART	SECOND PART	THIRD PART	FOURTH PART
The Gospels	**The Early Church**	**Paul's Life and his Letters**	**Various Letters & a Writing**
About Jesus.	Happenings after the Crucifixion.	Details of Paul's missionary journeys and his letters.	Letters from early Church leaders. One visionary writing.
Matthew Mark Luke John	Acts 1 to 8	Acts 9 to end Romans Corinthians I & II Galatians Ephesians * Philippians Colossians Thessalonians I & II Timothy I & II * Titus * Philemon	Hebrews James Peter I & II John I, II & III Jude Revelation (visionary writing)

There is some doubt that the letters of Paul marked * were written by Paul. They might have been written by others who used his name.

6 ABOUT THE GOSPELS

From the earliest age I can remember the excitement of getting a letter from the postman, opening the envelope and reading the message. Even now I enjoy receiving letters from friends I have not seen for some time, as I expect do most others. You can almost hear the writers talking to you and you can imagine what they were doing from just a few words of description. Because you know them and their ways you can fill in the bits which they did not say, and thereby understand better what they are telling you and how they felt.

In the same way the New Testament becomes more and more enriching and meaningful as we understand more about how and why each bit was written. As this learning continues we begin to understand better, and to see more clearly, what each author was getting at. We are less likely to read into the text something that is not there or to miss the important points.

The 27 books of the New Testament can be arranged into four sections.

-The first part tells us about Jesus. These are the gospels.
-The second part describes the New Church after the Crucifixion.
-The third part is an account of Paul's journeys and his letters.
-The fourth part is a collection of other letters and a visionary writing.

See opposite for a detailed breakdown.

It is not easy to imagine how the gospels arose as the circumstances two thousand years ago were so very different. In the very early days of the young Church the actions and teachings of Jesus would have been passed on from person to person by word of mouth.

Today, we have almost lost the art of story telling. We have no need for these skills as we have printed books, papers and photographs for reference. Extremely cheap writing materials make writing itself easy which in turn can be used as a quick aid to memory.

Story telling used to be a way of life and it survives today as a tradition in Punch and Judy shows, the Mystery Plays and nursery rhymes.

In olden times it was easier to remember all the tales handed down because there was not the flood of other things to distract and fill the mind. Today our brains are overworked trying to take in facts gushing from television, radio and the press.

We know that the stories about Jesus were not just confined to the Christian community. In Acts we find Peter saying to Cornelius the centurion, an officer in the occupying Roman army:

> You yourselves know that which was told throughout all Judaea, beginning from Galilee after the baptism which John preached; about Jesus of Nazareth ...   Acts 10:37,38

Most of the major cities had a stream of visiting Jews travelling abroad on business so the news could have been spread quite widely.

How the gospels came about may not seem relevant to what Jesus had to say, but it is important. You might plunge into the New Testament and it could speak to your condition straight away. On the other hand, you may be like myself, who at the start found little that made sense. It was as if I had dived blindly into a swimming pool and hit the bottom. How much better it would have been to have first looked beneath the water, studied the shape of the bottom, and then have jumped into a different place. If at the start I had understood how the New Testament was put together it would have been so much better.

Although the circumstances under which each of the gospels were written are different, we can see that there were four stages in which they came about although the dividing line between each stage is not clear.

STAGES OF WRITING THE GOSPELS

First stage	Oral tradition	What happened told by word of mouth.
Second stage	Proto-Gospels	Teaching material recorded and developed.
Third stage	Final writing	A full account assembled from many sources.

46

| Fourth stage | Re-editing | Later additions and amendments. |

ORAL HISTORY AND ORAL TRADITION

Oral History is the recounting of past events by someone who was there at the time. e.g. "When I was a child 80 years ago I remember seeing the King who had white hair."

Oral Tradition is the passing on of what other people have said. e.g. "Old Granny used to remember that the King had white hair."

Oral tradition, which worked like a grapevine where news went from person to person, should not be confused with sagas. The time when the history of past deeds had been handed down in the form of lengthy stories was long past; they had been replaced by written accounts such as in the Old Testament.

Archaeological research has shown that education was widespread and many could read although not so many could write. For letters and other documents the custom was to use scribes who were professional writers. This is the way Paul 'wrote' his letters as we can see from the end of his letter to the Corinthians. He was pleased to point out that he signed it himself:

'The salutation of me Paul with mine own hand.' 1 Corinthians 16:21

We must remember that in the early days of the church the end of the known world, the return of Jesus and the dawn of the new age, were expected at any moment. Any writings were used solely for teaching and spreading the news, and not for recording events for history. It was not until the hope of an immediate return started to fade that it was felt that there was a need for more permanent records.

Thus the second stage came about bit by bit as the preaching and spoken teaching material were written as notes. These notes were probably in many forms, such as a collection of the sayings of Jesus, but they were not an ordered or connected narrative (except possibly in the account of the Passion). They were proto-gospels, the forerunners or parents of the gospels.

It was much later that the third stage, a fuller account of Jesus

47

and his message came into being. The authors drew the material together from various sources, and gave it shape and order. Luke, who travelled with Paul in his missionary journeys, explains at the start of his gospel that he was doing just that. The disciples, as well as others including the women who followed Jesus, were all spreading the 'good news' but at this stage, as Luke says, the versions were not in a complete form.

Luke's gospel was probably the only one which was written as a book might be written today, with someone making a definite decision to sit down and to write. It is more likely that the other gospels evolved and grew over many years, in much the same way that your list of home telephone numbers developed. You start with a few numbers, add to them, then rewrite the list as it has become a bit of a mess because new numbers have been added and changes made.

If I asked you what date you wrote your telephone list you would think I was a bit strange. Thus with the gospels, the question as to when they were written is a non-question. So when we ask "When was a gospel written?" perhaps the question really means "When was it finally edited and put together?" It is almost impossible to find out what happened prior to that. Some scholars suggest that the gospels as we know them were put into circulation earlier than previously thought; maybe between 20 or 30 years after Jesus' death. The traditional view is that they were later, appearing between 30 and 70 years after the Crucifixion.

In much the same way the question of which author wrote first or copied or knew of the other gospels is also too rigid. There was much travelling and visiting between communities, and quite naturally the stories and early proto-gospels would have been discussed between church members. Some passages could have been shared between the different writings without having the original source in writing in front of the person or persons trying to put together a gospel.

Finally in the fourth stage, the gospels were re-edited, often with some bits added. We know this because the style of writing changes. In the case of John's gospel there are two endings. The first at the end of chapter 20, and the second in the final verses of chapter 21. Different people have very different ideas of why, by whom and when this final chapter was added. All the same, it does demonstrate how readily bits have been tacked on to the gospels.

Knowing how these writings came about helps us to understand them, but there are other things we need to keep in mind; such as poetry, language and humour.

Poetry has power and can bring out deep feelings and longings. The word 'Poetry' has a wider meaning than just written verse. Song, paintings, and even activities such as motorcycling can 'talk' to us in a way that is meaningful. Poetry can be a way of communicating and expressing the thoughts or feelings which are normally difficult to put into words.

Jesus taught in a kind of poetry and if, when we read the gospels, we look for and get the feel for that poetry, his teaching becomes alive and 'speaks' to us. He used many forms of poetry—stories, picture language, symbols.

We have been brought up with stories and are used to looking for the meaning behind them. For example, we hardly need the story of 'The Sower and the Seed' to be explained to us.

> "Behold, the sower went out to sow; and as he sowed, some seeds fell by the way side, and the birds came and devoured them: and others fell upon the rocky places, where they had not much earth; and straightway they sprang up, because they had no deepness of earth: and when the sun was risen, they were scorched; and because they had no root they withered away. And others fell among thorns; and the thorns grew up, and choked them: and others fell upon the good ground, and yielded fruit, some a hundredfold, some sixty, some thirty. He that has ears, let him hear."
>
> And the disciples came and said to him, "Why do you speak to them in parables?"   Matthew 13:3-9

Jesus in reply to this question explained that the disciples had been allowed to know the secrets of the Kingdom of Heaven, but others had not. He then went on to explain the meaning behind the story (verses 18 to 23). The disciples were not fools and, as the meaning is obvious, why did he have to explain it? Jesus was using it as an example of how they should teach. One of the best ways to put over an idea is to illustrate the point with a story.

You will also notice that 'The Sower and the Seed' has an extra bit at the end. Jesus often added a final unexpected twist or finished by exaggerating. These end pieces bring out the message more forcibly because the visual image is enhanced. In this case the image we get is of the seed not only germinating and bearing

49

fruit, but increasing by so much even a 'hundredfold'.

Not all the stories are easy and straightforward to understand. The ones directed at particular people or circumstances can appear puzzling to us today unless we look back to Bible times.

One of the most difficult to understand —'The Rich Man and the Dishonest Steward'— becomes clear when we realise that when Jesus talks about 'the children of light' he is not referring to his followers but to the Essenes and their absolute rigidity. It has an important message for the churches today; not to worry about rules and regulations but to get down to the job of caring for as many people as possible. The story with its message is summarised in the box opposite.

There is another form of poetry which is not commonly accepted as such today and which can seem quite strange if you have not come across it before. However, once you get used to it, it adds to the pleasure and interest of the Bible. It is the poetry of repeated ideas or thoughts, and these repeated ideas can be in many different patterns.

The Old Testament prophets in the Bible are shown to speak in this way. Here is an example from the Old Testament. The different ideas are shown in the first column and the letters A, B, and C stand for each idea.

Introduction	Woe unto them
Idea A	that decree unrighteous decrees
repeat A	and to the writers that write evil:
Idea B	to stop the needy from getting judgement
repeat B	and to take away the rights of the poor,
Idea C	that widows may be their plunder
repeat C	and make the fatherless their prey!
	Isaiah 10:1-2

The thoughts in the last two lines —Idea C— on first sight do not look the same. In fact they are, since taking from widows or orphans would have been disastrous as both would have had to live off other people's kindness.

Repeated thoughts can include the reversing of ideas. First one idea is put forward and then the converse or other way round is mentioned. For example:

Idea A	A - A	They are bowed down and fallen:
(a is converse of A)	a - a	But we are risen and stand upright.
		Psalm 20:8

50

The Rich Man and the Dishonest Steward
Luke 16:1-12

The story, which is told to the disciples, is about a wealthy man who had a steward who was managing the estate badly. On being told that he was to be dismissed for incompetence, the steward went to those owing money to the estate and demanded only a proportion back. Because he let them off some of the debt, they in turn would give him something to live off after he was sacked.

For us today this is dishonest, but surprisingly, in the story the steward was praised by the rich man for being clever. Jesus goes on to say that the Children of this World are wiser than the Children of Light.

In those days there were no banks as we understand them today. If you had any surplus cash, you lent it to others who made use of it. For example, goods might be bought cheaply in one country and shipped for sale in another, and if there was a profit at the end it was shared with you.

It was the steward's job to manage the rich man's money, and this steward was not good at chasing-up people to make sure that he got the profits at the end. So when he was told that he was going to be sacked, he started to get as much back as he could. He did this by doing a deal with the debtors so encouraging them to release any cash they had.

He was cutting the losses, which was a sensible thing to do, and was therefore praised by the rich man. If he had been strict and demanded all the moneys back there and then, there would have been problems and difficulties. Much of the money had been re-invested and was not available. Not only was he doing the best for the rich man, but he was also putting himself in a good position for later.

The key to the message is in the last sentence of the story. Jesus says that the Children of this World (Jesus and his disciples) are wiser than the Children of Light (The Essenes). We know from the Dead Sea Scrolls that Children of Light was one of the names the Essenes gave themselves. They were most strict in the way they lived; any member who did not keep the Law of Moses was expelled from the community and certainly not thought to be acceptable to God.

The purpose of the story now becomes clear; it is a policy statement for the disciples on how they should go about their work.

In the past the religious leaders had been inefficient at getting God's message across. The disciples must live in this world, and make the best of a bad job by bringing into the fold as many people as possible without worrying about their imperfections. This policy is wiser than the Essene way, which insists on one hundred percent correctness, thus excluding many.

51

In the Old Testament there are books which are just poetry: The Psalms, Song of Songs and Lamentations. The New Testament also contains poetry of repeated ideas, such as in The Sermon on The Mount (Matthew chapters 5 to 7). In this example there is an action followed by the outcome. This is then repeated but with a new idea:-

(a follows from A)	A - a	Ask and it shall be given you;
(b follows from B)	B - b	Seek, and you shall find;
(c follows from C)	C - c	Knock, and it shall be opened to you.

The cycle is next repeated but with the meaning slightly changed:-

(a follows from A)	A - a	For everyone that asks receives,
(b follows from B)	B - b	And he that seeks finds,
(c follows from C)	C - c	And to him that knocks, it shall be opened.

Matthew 7:7-8

Many of Jesus' sayings have come down to us in poetry. Perhaps one of the reasons why he was recognised as a prophet could have been that he used poetry as part of his teaching as did the prophets.

Some questions often asked are about the actual words Jesus used. 'Do we know for sure what Jesus really said?' 'How accurate is the Bible in quoting him?' 'What language did he use?'

At the time there were four major languages spoken in the Holy Land.

Aramaic	The language in use in Galilee which was Jesus' native language. Some of the Dead Sea Scrolls were written in Aramaic.
Greek	A language in common use among most of the well educated.
Hebrew	The old language of the Jews which was their classic language of religion.
Latin	Used in the Roman empire and was the language of the occupying army.

There are so many things around us which we normally cannot see or touch but which we understand and take for granted in our everyday life. Radio, electricity, beams which turn our TVs on and off, germs which can make us ill, and many more. In the same way we have many concepts or ideas which are abstract, ideas such as 'history', 'virtue', 'experience', 'religion', 'nature' and 'conscience'.

There were few abstract words in the ancient Hebrew culture of the Old Testament and the words just listed did not exist in their language.

The people lived in a very direct way where everything that happened was on account of God. That God 'loved' or 'hated' was not how God felt toward the person but was what happened to the person. To be at 'peace' did not mean some peaceful idea but denoted that you were 'doing very nicely thank you'. God made a 'covenant' with the Jews, which just meant that God would protect the Jewish race and see that they were 'OK', provided they kept his 'laws'. The 'Law' in turn was a practical list of dos and don'ts, rather than a moral code.

If we think of countries today in which many languages are spoken we will note that the population is multi-lingual. Unlike the English-speaking world it is not unusual for many to be quite fluent in two, three or even four languages. There is no reason to suppose that Jesus would have been any different, and furthermore he could not have conversed with such a wide range of folk if he were not multi-lingual.

There are difficulties in deciding whether a particular passage in the Bible mirrors the actual words of Jesus.

Problems at the time of Jesus

- We are unsure which language Jesus was using at any one time.
- Jesus left no writings so we can only guess at his style of speech.
- People may not have remembered correctly his exact words.
- The sayings may have changed as they were passed on from person to person.

Problems during writing the New Testament

- Jesus probably taught the crowds in Aramaic which could have been incorrectly translated into Greek.

- The sayings could have been edited by the writers or changed by the early church to fit their ideas.
- Writing many years after the life of Jesus reduces accuracy of the words.

Problems today

- The meanings of words change as time goes on and the interpretation of some original Greek words is guesswork.
- There may not be a word or phrase in existence which gives the flavour of the original word used. For instance Jesus often used puns, words which had two meanings, and which are difficult or impossible to translate.

In spite of all these difficulties there are some words which Jesus probably used:

- *"Eloi, Eloi, lama sabachthani?"*, which is being interpreted, 'My God, my God, why hast thou forsaken me?' Mark 15:34 & Psalm 22
- *"Talitha cumi"* which is being interpreted 'Damsel, I say to you, Arise.' Mark 5:41

These are the only two passages which quote Jesus in Aramaic, and therefore it is a good bet that they reflected his actual words. Also it is likely that he had an unusual way of starting his sentences:

- *"Amen, I say to you"*, in the synoptic gospels.
  or
- *"Amen, Amen, I say to you"* in John.

The statement occurs frequently, 30 times in Matthew, 13 in Mark, 6 in Luke and 25 in John. Normally prayers finished with 'Amen', meaning certainty, but Jesus started off like this, meaning that what he was about to say was truly what God wanted.

The phrase is translated in many ways: 'Truly ...', 'Verily ...', 'I am telling you the truth', 'Tell most solemnly', 'Mark my words', 'Believe me', 'I tell you this'.

Another characteristic of Jesus which has received little attention is his humour. We are so used to taking the Bible seriously that we seldom look for the jokes or the funny quips. We do not often think of Jesus as a jovial character wining and dining with all. He was certainly not a boring speaker, and often used humour to make his point.

Whether you get a laugh out of your audience or not depends so much on the facial expression, the voice intonation and the timing for the occasion. But when the words which have caused amusement are put into writing they can become utterly flat. It is not easy to reconstruct the original joviality and any attempt requires great imagination, something we need to cultivate in our study of the Bible.

The humour of Jesus was never at the expense of others, not like today when so much in the media is cruel. Jesus did not jeer at human frailty, but he used humorous exaggeration to make his point.

In Matthew he 'ticks off' the lawyers and Pharisees, who are the moral leaders of the nation. They calculate their tax gifts to the temple even in herbs whilst neglecting basic justice and mercy. He says:

> You blind guides, which strain out the gnat, and swallow a camel!
> Matthew 23:24

When telling someone who is wealthy to turn from material things, how could you do better than say with a large smile:-

> It is easier for a camel to go through a needle's eye than for a rich man to enter the kingdom of God.　　　Mark 10:25

When reading the gospels we can get more out of them if we watch out for and enjoy the poetry and humour.

THE OLD PROPHETS SPOKE ON BEHALF OF GOD.
HOW DO WE KNOW WHEN GOD SPEAKS TO US TODAY?

There had been many leaders and prophets in the history of the Jews, and they saw themselves as speaking on behalf of God telling the people what God wanted. For instance Moses told of the ten commandments, Elijah's message was the need to drive out foreign Gods, and Amos that God requires social action. Jesus was part of this tradition and he was accepted by his hearers as speaking from God.

Today we are more doubtful of the idea of God speaking to us, or telling us things. There are two questions which come up.

Firstly, in what way does God speak to someone? Is it in a voice, is it in a dream, or is it that we just suddenly know that we have received God's word? The answer is that it is different for different people, and it is good that we are all different.

In most cases it is that we just 'know'. Perhaps a feeling has been slowly building up over years. It is this 'just knowing' that we must be alive to, and listen to. Some people are more tuned in and find it easier than others. We need to be like a guitar string that is tuned to the right pitch and in resonance.

Secondly, how do we know that it is God telling us? How do we know that we are not just inventing things, not on purpose but as a result of our subconscious mind? Maybe as a result of the things around us? This is important as so many people through the ages have been led astray by a wrong idea, by a wrong notion that it was God telling them to do something. To them it might have seemed right but to everyone else it was obviously wrong and evil. Killing and torturing in the name of religion has been happening since history started. The answer may be simple:

'By their fruits you shall know them'   Matthew 7:20

It is from God if the result is good and if it gives spiritual help and well-being to others. But if it increases our own satisfaction that we are doing a good job, even a good job for our church which inwardly we feel smug about, then more than likely it is not God-sent. Although the answer seems simple, to listen and cut out the clatter of daily life is difficult.

56

7 THE SYNOPTIC GOSPELS AND JOHN

Some people are disappointed and bored to find that the first three gospels —Matthew, Mark and Luke— say the same thing. At first sight reading one is much like reading another, and there is very little in Mark that is not in Matthew and Luke. Mark contains only 31 verses out of a total of 661 which are not in either of the other two.

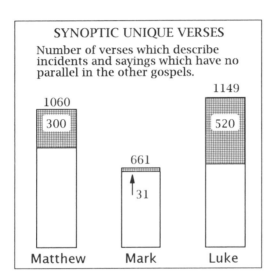

The three gospels Matthew, Mark and Luke are known as the synoptic gospels (from the Greek syn = same; optic = seeing) as they see the events in the same way. You could say that they are like three similar flowers of different colour in one vase. John's gospel is different as it tells an entirely different story. It is a flowering plant in a pot on its own.

Even though the three synoptic gospels seem the same and tell the story of Jesus in much the same way, they are different. Each author has taken up the tradition of Jesus in a particular way, and we can see the different aspects coming out which we would not otherwise have known.

The group of disciples from which the gospel of Matthew came concentrated on the Jewish tradition as they were working amongst Jews. The Mark and Luke schools emphasised the way Jesus appealed to all races as they were working amongst Greek and Roman converts.

Here is a summary of some of the more important facts about each gospel, but remember that historical information of this type is just speculation. The earlier dates proposed by John Robinson have been used rather than the more widely accepted later dating.

THE GOSPEL WRITINGS

Gospel: **MATTHEW**
Traditional Author/Editor: Someone from the 'school' led by Matthew, the disciple who was a tax-gatherer.
Where: Antioch in Syria or Alexandria in Egypt.
Main Source: Collection of sayings over a long period of time.
Writing style: Correct, although not exceptionally inspired, Greek.
Possible Date of First Draft: AD 40 to 50.   *Possible Final Draft:* 60 to 70.
Community being written for: Jewish Christians.
Underlying theme: Jesus is the promised Messiah and a true Jew. Arguments for use with other Jews.
Circumstances of writing: Because the gospel was a long time in being formed it contains some of the earliest material as well as later traditions. Sections could have been copied from Mark.

Gospel: **MARK**
Traditional Author/Editor: John Mark, mentioned in Acts and who worked with Paul.
Where: Rome and then Alexandria in Egypt.
Main Source of information: Peter before his martyrdom.
Writing style: Straightforward and simple Greek with traces of Aramaic, perhaps directly from Peter.
Possible Date of First Draft: AD 50 to 60.   *Possible Final Draft:* 60 to 70.
Community being written for: Christians of Roman origin living in Rome.
Underlying theme: The events are put together as a dramatic story. It is the Gospel of action and Jesus' power to save.
Circumstances of writing: Could have started in Rome and tradition has it that Mark moved to Egypt during the persecutions and finished it there.

Gospel: LUKE
Traditional Author/Editor: Luke companion of Paul.
Where: A city such as Corinth.
Main Source: Paul and Antioch Christians, also maybe material from Philip in Caesarea.
Writing style: Polished and elegant Greek writing.
Possible Date of First Draft: AD 55 to 60.   *Possible Final Draft:* 60 to 70.
Community being written for: Non-Jewish Christians such as those converted by Paul.
Underlying theme: Christians are good citizens and the Roman authorities have no need to fear them. Jesus is the friend of the underdog, the poor and the outcast.
Circumstances of writing: Draws together the many sources and accounts of Jesus.

Gospel: JOHN
Traditional Author/Editor: A John we know little about, maybe a youth at the Crucifixion. Many names have been suggested: John Zebedee, a son of John Zebedee, John Mark, the son of Caiaphas the High Priest or a son of John the Baptist.
Where: Ephesus.
Main Source: Eyewitness or close to an eyewitness.
Writing style: Simple Greek as it was spoken rather than written.
Possible Date of First Draft: AD 35 to 50.   *Possible Final Draft:* 70 to 100.
Community being written for: Christians in Ephesus.
Underlying theme: Actual record and inner meanings of Jesus' teaching.
Circumstances of writing: Originally for local converts emphasising the nature of Jesus' teaching.

It is unlikely that these early sayings and stories would have given a complete picture of the life and message of Jesus. Imagine what happens when you go to see a film or play that is humorous but with a serious message. The funny bits are immediately impressed in your mind. Afterwards you come home and tell your friends about it and you will naturally repeat those funny bits first. Only later will you ponder and discuss the more serious side and repeat them. In the long run these ideas could influence you the most.

Jesus built his teaching on stories, parables and sayings which would stick in the mind and then later the deeper meaning could come out. Thus the parables and the most striking activities of Jesus were the first bits to go into the oral tradition; the deeper thoughts and messages were passed on at a later time.

The synoptic gospels contain a great number of the stories

and actions whilst in the Gospel of John the deeper message is told. These two boxes show in a simplified graphical form how the gospels may have come about.

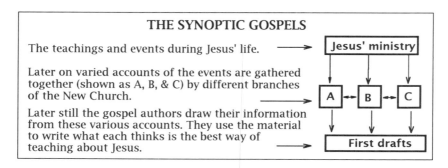

The synoptic gospels were, and still are, an excellent way of teaching about Jesus, because they group together the material in a convenient and simple manner. They are like photographs or video recordings of instances in the life of Jesus that, after being jumbled up, years later have been strung together in a simple order. The object was to emphasise plainly what he said and did through his parables and actions. Indeed, this is just what Jesus intended as his sayings and parables were directed at the multitudes of ordinary people, the 'am ha-aretz.

The gospel of John is different, it is one person's version of what happened.

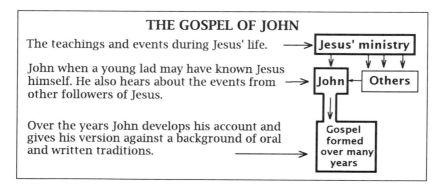

The general opinion is that the Gospel of John was put into circulation many years after the other gospels. Scholars differ over the date, some say it was just after AD 70 and others around AD 100. Whatever the date it could have been in its present form for many years, gradually evolving during John's lifetime. It was John's personal way of preaching and teaching to his followers. Just after he died it could have been written up and published with the addition of the last chapter. As usual the evidence is meagre and open to different interpretations.

Whilst the synoptic gospels are like a series of photographs put into an order to make a simple story, the Gospel of John is like theatre. When reading John it can be helpful to imagine that we are watching a play where the important aspects of the thinking and life of Jesus are brought out. Plays often tell the public about famous people and what they were trying to achieve. It is a good way of showing what the person was really thinking and doing, and also portrays the circumstances which forced the person to do what he or she did. There are many plays that do this: Shakespearean historical dramas and plays set in countries with racial tension such as South Africa.

The problem is that there are major differences in the life of Jesus as told by the synoptic gospels and John. Some examples are:-

SOME DIFFERENCES IN THE ACCOUNTS OF THE LIFE OF JESUS	
Synoptic Account	**Johannine Account**
Jesus' ministry lasts one year and he visits Jerusalem only at the very end.	Jesus makes four visits during a two year ministry.
The Last Supper described in Mark (14.12) was the Passover Meal.	The Last Supper is before the Passover festival. (John 13.1)
The Cleansing of the Temple, when Jesus drives out the traders, occurs just before the Crucifixion. (Mark 11.15)	The Cleansing of the Temple occurs at the start of the ministry two years before the Crucifixion. (John 2.14)

Which sequence of events are we to take as more likely to be nearer the actual truth? The simple and straightforward account of the synoptic gospels? Or the complex record by John which could be mistaken as it is only one person's view? The question is more than just one of interest; the answer will colour how we interpret the sayings of Jesus.

I have never been comfortable with the historical life of Jesus as put forward in the synoptic gospels. Somehow it did not seem to fit in with what Jesus was doing and the events going on around him. The ministry seemed too short to achieve so much, and why did the centre of activity shift to Jerusalem after the Crucifixion if he only made the one brief final visit? For many years these doubts were the major reason that made me suspicious of the whole New Testament. Not so now; the story of what happened and why Jesus was doing things falls into place. This comes about when John is taken as being more likely to be right when there is a difference between the Johannine and synoptic versions.

There are two main reasons why John should be taken as the correct account. Firstly, the happenings in John do not fit into the synoptic story.

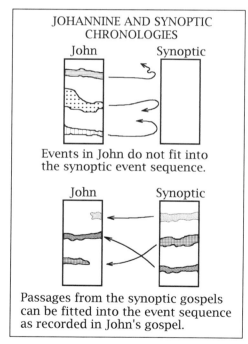

JOHANNINE AND SYNOPTIC
CHRONOLOGIES
John   Synoptic

Events in John do not fit into
the synoptic event sequence.

John   Synoptic

Passages from the synoptic gospels
can be fitted into the event sequence
as recorded in John's gospel.

For example, Jesus' teaching in the temple during the autumn

62

feast of Tabernacles, told in John chapter 5, cannot be fitted into any of the synoptic gospel time frames. They only tell of Jesus making one visit to Jerusalem and that was in the spring at his final Passover. But the happenings in the synoptic gospels can be fitted into John's account. For instance, the temptation of Jesus in the wilderness could have happened during April/May of the first year of Jesus' ministry as depicted by John.

Those people who assume that the synoptic history is more likely to be correct talk about John moving the episodes to suit his presentation. It makes more sense to assume that John knew what Jesus did and built his explanations and theology around that.

Secondly, the synoptic gospels are mostly vague when talking of places and times. The writers seem not to have had a deep knowledge of Palestine. John when writing about events in and around Jerusalem is often precise, giving the names of villages visited and the time it took to travel between them. We can see this happening in the story about Martha and Mary. Luke is vague:

Now as they were on there way, he entered into a certain village: and a certain woman named Martha received him into her house. And she had a sister called Mary ...   Luke 10:38

but in John the village Bethany is clearly stated to be nearly two miles from Jerusalem:

Bethany was near to Jerusalem, about two miles off; and many of the Jews had come to Martha and Mary to console them concerning brother's death.   John 11:19

Although the synoptic gospels do not give exact places and times of what Jesus was doing, they give vital information. Like photographs they give a clear picture of separate events and, when fitted into John's gospel they fill it out adding to it in a convincing way.

As a result I now see that the force and breadth of Jesus' teaching is more powerful than I could have thought possible.

LIFE IS FULL OF LINKS

In the Fourth Gospel almost all the happenings in the life of Jesus are used by the author to bring out some theological point or to reflect a passage from the Jewish scripture. It is natural to assume that most of John's Gospel is a result of creative writing to suit the point he was trying to make. We can say 'The chances that the incidents were really like that are very low because they fit so well.' Indeed many scholars take this view.

I think that this is wrong, and that the gospel is not just fiction. There is no need to believe that John was making up the gospel events. All the same, as we have already seen, he was writing how he thought the characters would have spoken, but that is no reason to doubt that the incidents had a historical base.

We try to make sense of our surroundings by creating connections between things. There are a great number of combinations of events in life and if one looks for coincidences they are there.

To illustrate the point let me tell you of a little game I play. I look at my horoscopes in the popular press and use them in the wrong way.

I read the 'forecast' and find links with the things that have happened in the past. These 'forecasts' seem to be accurate in telling the past. This is because the meaning of words can be stretched and fitted to at least one of the many past events. 'Have money problems' can be taken as not finding that penny in your purse for change as well as having no money!

We all know that these matches arise from chance resulting from the range of happenings in one's daily life and the many interpretations which can be placed on them.

In much the same way people in New Testament times were looking for the links with scripture to tell them what God was saying, and were finding them. It was these links that were passed on from person to person as oral tradition.

8 THE GOSPEL OF JOHN

The Gospel of John tells us a great deal about Jesus. It contains a high proportion —about 85%— of original material and even when the theological statements in the prologue and discourses are excluded the proportion is still high at 80%.

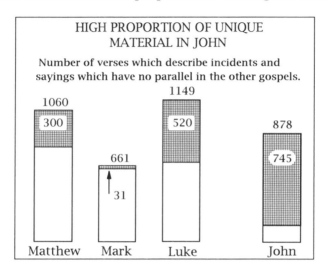

HIGH PROPORTION OF UNIQUE
MATERIAL IN JOHN

Number of verses which describe incidents and
sayings which have no parallel in the other gospels.

Why should John contain so much unique material? Perhaps the author was teaching what he knew about Jesus against the already well known background of the synoptic gospels. He was putting the record straight as to what he thought actually occurred as well as focusing on the message which the others covered less adequately. There would have been no benefit in him repeating all the teaching material contained in the other gospels.

At the same time he had a problem. He had to tell his 'true' story of the life and message of Jesus without seeming to be attacking the other gospels and causing divisions within the Christian community. He could not say directly that they were wrong, he could only show that he knew the facts by quoting detail. As stated at the end of the gospel 'His witness is true'.

Here are two examples of the way he corrects what he sees as wrong in the other accounts.

The first example is that both Matthew and Luke clearly state that Jesus was born in Bethlehem. (Mark does not cover the birth events at all.) The only time John refers to the birth of Jesus is in an indirect way. A crowd is arguing if Jesus is the Christ;

> Others said "This is the Christ". But some said, "What, does the Christ come out of Galilee? Has not the scripture said that the Christ comes from the seed of David, and from Bethlehem, the village where David was?" John 7:41-42

The author John is showing that Jesus did not come from King David's city of Bethlehem and therefore was not a warrior leader as was King David.

The second example is the role of John the Baptist. The synoptic gospels depict him in a simple way as the one who baptised Jesus. They had to do it like this as they, especially Mark and Luke, were written to teach 'Christianity' to converts, such as those who lived in Rome, who knew little about Judaism. To go into any other explanation would have been too complicated and would have detracted from the job for which they were written.

The Fourth Gospel approaches the subject of the Baptist in a different way. The object of the author was to tell the true story even if it made the writing more difficult to grasp. He does not mention the baptism of Jesus, although he assumes it. Instead —as we shall see in the next chapter— he sets the Baptist in the more complex and plausible role of the traditional Jewish prophet revealing the Messiah. To do this required much detail and lengthy explanations. The first 42 verses of John describe the theology and role of the Baptist. In Mark's gospel it is only the first 12 verses which are needed to tell about the Baptist and the baptism of Jesus.

It is interesting to note how the author John emphasises that the Baptist was not the Messiah. This is repeated time and time again —ten times in chapter 1 as well as in chapters 3, 5 and 10— and it is typical of the way John uses repetition when he wants to make a point.

Why does he seem to be so obsessed with the fact that it was Jesus who was the Messiah rather than the Baptist? Maybe because some believed the Baptist was the true Messiah, and we know that he had a large number of devotees. Also, it could have been possible that some Christian converts whom the author knew had reverted and become followers of the Baptist once more. Had that been so, it would have caused the author considerable pain resulting in the need to stress that the Messiah was Jesus.

The Gospel of John is the most difficult gospel to understand because it works at many different levels in subtle ways. It is this which makes it so rewarding to study. Here are some characteristics.

- It is a great mythical-dramatic statement which is also grounded in the sound knowledge of the life of Jesus and of the geography around Jerusalem.

- It is uniform in style (except perhaps chapter 21).

- The themes are consistent throughout.

- It is not in a final form. It is disjointedly written with parts having been added without full editing e.g. chapters 15, 16 and 17.

- The exact meaning of many words is ignored and instead they are used to mean something else. e.g. Nicodemus being *born* of the Spirit. These metaphors require knowledge of the culture at the time in order to enable us to sort out better the dividing line between metaphors and real life.

- Many parallels are drawn and references made back to the scriptures in ways which are not at first sight obvious.

- The words of Jesus often follow the feast day readings from particular sections of the Jewish Bible.

- There is much symbolism. Numbers are often significant. e.g. 5 –there are five books of Moses; 7 –God created the world in seven days in Genesis; 12 –the twelve tribes of Israel.

- There are 7 miracles, or signs as they are called, each one giving a special message. They are graduated with each one being more powerful than the previous one.

As we read John we find that the sayings of Jesus get longer and longer. These speeches, or discourses, were not meant to tell us what Jesus actually said, quoting him word for word. They follow the custom of the time where writers put long speeches into the mouths of the characters to demonstrate feelings. Today we go to a play by Shakespeare and hear the characters telling of

67

their hopes and fears in the same way.

John wrote what he thought Jesus would have said. Beside this, John probably knew Jesus and remembered him speaking, so the way Jesus spoke and in some places what he actually said could have been included. As a result we get a strange mixture of:
  (1) what John remembered, and was told of, the words of Jesus
  (2) what John thought Jesus would have said
and it is not easy to separate one from another.

John was interpreting the spiritual or mystical message of Jesus as he —John— saw it, which is almost impossible to put into words. For us to understand that message, we need to do something which is not easy for those of us brought up in the Western world. We need to remove our language ability and let the spirit take over. We need, as we saw in the first chapter of this book, to get behind the words.

Here is a summary in very broad terms what I think John was saying, and it is only a guide to start you off on your own journey. You will only be able to make up your own mind if you are in contact with the writing, and then you will get the feel of the spirit which has fired so many over the years.

1. SPIRITUAL BOND WITH GOD

'For I speak not from myself, but the Father which sent me, he has given me a commandment, what I should say, and what I should speak. And I know that his commandment is life eternal.'   John 12:49-50

'Let not your heart be troubled: believe in God, believe also in me.'
John 14:1

'Do you not believe that I am in the Father, and the Father in me? The words that I say to you I speak not from myself: but the Father living in me does his works.'   John 14:10

Jesus had a very close spiritual bond with God. It is this closeness to God which matters above all else. It mattered in Jesus' lifetime and it matters now. It matters in all our actions, in our daily life, and even when we feel down and useless. During such moments of despair, when nothing seems to be going right, we still need to be attached to that spirit of God even if the thread holding us appears to be gossamer thin.

John makes it clear that it is our choice.

2. SPIRITUAL BOND WITH ALL

A new commandment I give you, that you love one another; even as I have loved you, that you also love one another. By this shall all people know that you are my disciples, if you have love one for another.
John 13:34-35

This spiritual bond we have includes everybody, it is like a circle with all middle and no edge. We sometimes call it love, not a liking or sexual love, but a deep at-oneness with everyone. We can sense the presence of God within our most hated enemies. This love will come out and show itself in the way we get on with other people. Not that we need to be close friends with everyone we meet, but we need to respect others as having the spirit of God in them. I often feel that there is an inner spirit of goodness trying to get out of me which I hold in because of myself. Somehow it is locked in by how I am. We may all be like that, hating ourselves for not letting the spirit blossom. We need to look for that spirit in others too.

3. READY FOR THE END

'This is the work of God: that you believe on him whom he has sent.'
John 6:29

'For I came not to judge the world, but to save the world.' John 12:47

'For this is the will of my Father, that every one that sees the Son, and believes on him, should have eternal life; and I will raise him up at the last day.'
John 6:40

The world as it was, with its evil and unhappiness, was thought to be about to end at any moment. Jesus knew that he was the person who spoke on behalf of God. He was to get people ready for the new age or kingdom where everything would be perfect. This readiness was a total acceptance of God in a spiritual way.

4. LEAVING THE WORLD IN ORDER TO RETURN

'I shall go away, and you shall seek me, and you shall die in your sin: where I go you cannot come.'
John 8:21

'A little while, and you will see me no more; and again a little while, and you shall see me.'
John 16:16

> 'I came out from the Father, and am come into the world: again, I leave the world and go to the Father'. John 16:28

Jesus knew that, at the end when God would intervene, he would have to go and come back. He did not know exactly how; that was in God's hands. He might have to suffer in some way, as predicted by the prophet Isaiah 700 years before.

5. RETURNING TO THE SECOND CREATION

> 'And if I go and prepare a place for you, I shall come again, and will receive you to myself; that where I am, there you may be also. And where I go, you know the way.' John 14:3-4

> 'But I will see you again, and your heart shall rejoice, and your joy no one will take away from you.' John 16:22

Jesus, as the Messiah, would return to the new world to do what was wanted. Maybe he would be judging, maybe he would be leading and organising in the new society. Again, how it would work out was God's business; it was not necessary to know exactly what would happen.

6. CONCLUSION: THE DECISION IS YOURS

> 'He that believeth on the Son has eternal life; but he that obeys not the Son shall not see life.' John 3:36

The Jesus of John invites rather than teaches. Everyone has the choice to be on the one hand 'of this world' —'in darkness', 'be blind', 'hate the light', or 'see death'— and on the other 'from above' —'believe in me', have 'light', 'truth', 'life in his name'.

But it all started with John the Baptist.

ETERNAL LIFE
'Eternal Life' is not living a worldly life for ever, but a spiritual 'life' outside time.

WISDOM AND THE WORD

WISDOM

In Old Testament times there were a number of ways in which God let you know about 'himself' and what was required of you. There was the Law which was recorded in The Five Books of Moses together with interpretations, there were the prophets who spoke on behalf of God, and there was a third way – the reason 'why and wherefore' of the universe. It was called Wisdom or *Sophia* in Greek and formed a central part of the thinking and was equivalent to scientific reasoning today.

At the time it was thought that human conduct could alter the balance of the cosmic forces. An act done at the wrong time could have bad consequences. Therefore wise sayings pointing to the regularities of life and nature were listed in order to codify or to set in order the way of the world. The books of wisdom in the Old Testament —Job, Proverbs and Ecclesiastes— and especially Ecclesiasticus in the Apocrypha list these truisms.

Wisdom was personified, being presented as a female semi-angel figure, who lived in heaven and covered the earth as a mist. She was not God but a part of God. Her function was, so to speak, like the governor of the school of life who taught and guided the correct way to behave.

> She is more precious than rubies: And none of the things you can desire are to be compared unto her.

> Length of days is in her right hand; In her left hand are riches and honour.   Proverbs 3:15-16

The Fourth Gospel draws on concepts from the Wisdom literature.

THE WORD

The Word, *Logos* in Greek, is a similar concept to Wisdom, but it conveys the idea of the action of God speaking, telling or communicating. John used the term to describe the relationship of God and Jesus and explain that God was made known through Jesus. As with 'Wisdom', 'The Word' portrayed a part of God.

Had John said that Jesus was God he would have been blaspheming as that would have been unacceptable to the Jews.

71

PART 2

THE STORY OF JESUS
AS TOLD BY JOHN

THE RIVER JORDAN

View of the Jordan not far from where it flows into
the Sea of Galilee. Tradition has it that baptisms
were carried out somewhere on this stretch of river,
although it is not the place mentioned in the
gospels.

9 JOHN THE BAPTIST

Water has a way of making us feel at peace, whether we are lying in the bath, swimming, or even looking at a puddle. Hearing the thunder of waves breaking or just watching a flowing stream makes the cares of the world seem unimportant. The river Jordan has the same effect as it winds its way through the desert lands, and today pilgrims still come from afar to be baptised in the river.

Some years ago during a visit to Galilee someone asked our guide to take us somewhere to swim. After some hesitation he said, "All right, I'll take you to a place on the Jordan river". So we arrived at a car park which to our surprise was packed with row upon row of coaches. We got out, walked down the steep bank to the sluggish river and were met with the sight of pilgrims from various lands being immersed in the water. Many were splendid gnarled and broadly beaming peasant women, some from Greece or Cyprus. Some had beautiful white embroidered cloth shrouds which would be used at their burial, and one old lady, even older and seemingly poorer than the rest, had only a white vest instead of a more elaborate shroud. It was their lifelong ambition to be baptised in the Jordan before they died.

We were much moved by this activity and all thoughts of our swim disappeared. My wife had a small bottle which she filled with Jordan water to take home; the best things are often the cheapest!

It was on the banks of the Jordan that John the Baptist was preaching and baptising. The river must have given an extra spiritual dimension to his preaching.

The gospels are meant to be about Jesus, so why all this fuss about John the Baptist? Why is he given so much attention in all the gospels and in Acts? Surely there must be more to it than the routine answer we are often given that 'He was the person who baptised Jesus'? The answer is 'Yes, there is more to it' if we believe the events as told by John's gospel are as close to the truth as we can get. The lives of John the Baptist and Jesus were closely linked.

John the Baptist was a mighty prophet spreading his message to the enraptured crowds which flocked to him. He must have been an outstanding person, for they did not trudge through the wilderness just to watch the reeds by the river's edge blowing in the wind.

The garment a person is wearing is not often mentioned in the New Testament, but in Matthew chapter 3 we have a picturesque description of the Baptist in his rough coat of camel's hair held in place with a leather belt. It is easy to visualise him with his thin face weather-beaten from living rough and feeding on foods gathered in the wild; he was no fat and flabby guru. For him was the austere life followed by the Essenes and other holy men.

WAS JOHN THE BAPTIST AN ESSENE?

Some people think that it is possible that John the Baptist was an Essene as they had much in common:-

- -Both led austere lives.
- -Both thought that the Messiah and the Kingdom would come at any moment.
- -Both thought that baptism by water was provisional. When the new age arrived it would be replaced by baptism by the Holy Spirit.

It has been suggested that he was one of the monks living at Qumran, and because he felt so strongly that the new age was about to start at any moment he had to leave to tell everyone. This could explain why he was living on wild food. As an Essene one of the vows he would have had to make was not to eat food cooked by others.

On the other hand, it was common for holy men to go into the desert and live extremely simply.

Perhaps he just had some association with the Essenes. He might have joined for a short period in his youth as did Josephus the Jewish historian. Maybe his family were connected with the lay movement.

We know from Mark's gospel that John the Baptist was immensely popular with a large following. After the chief priests asked Jesus by what authority he was acting Jesus answered:-

"The baptism of John: was it from heaven or from men? Answer me." And they reasoned with themselves, saying, "If we shall say 'From Heaven'; he will say, 'Then why did you not believe him?' But should we say, 'From men —'." They feared the people: for all held that John was a prophet.   Mark 11:30-32

Even the chief priests were afraid of the popular reaction if they were to cast any doubts on the truth behind the mission, and this incident occurred sometime after John the Baptist had been murdered by King Herod. Therefore his popularity was no short-lived matter.

The movement must have been quite large with followers spreading far and wide. In The Acts of the Apostles (19:1-4) we read that there were followers of the Baptist at Ephesus in Turkey when Paul arrived there in about AD 51.

What was the Baptist's message and why did he have such an impact? He was preaching strong stuff, pulling no punches, and being extremely rude to the well-to-do, telling them that they were a race of deadly poisonous snakes. He had the ability to inspire people into action with his words. He was a prophet, someone who spoke on behalf of God, and the message was forceful yet simple:–

"Repent; for the kingdom of heaven is at hand!"   Matt. 3:2

Repent meant not just to be sorry. You had to change your ways, heart and mind. If you didn't —be warned— you would be like a tree which does not give good fruit; it is cut down and burnt.

WHAT WILL HAPPEN TO THE WICKED?

It was not just the Baptist who was using strong language. The Dead Sea Scrolls tell that all who walk in the way of falsehood will be subject to the rage of God. Many different plagues will be sent by the destroying angels and also the wicked will be condemned to everlasting damnation, torment and disgrace.

It was no good thinking that just because you were a leading Jew descended from Abraham you would automatically be admitted into the new Garden of Eden. You had to change, and the change was to live according to the Jewish law in both your actions and in your attitudes.

But the need to change was urgent. The new happy age with no evil was starting at that very time. One can feel the excitement of expectation and the conviction that they were living at a critical moment when John the Baptist says:–

"And even now is the axe laid at the root of the trees." Matt. 3:10

77

The process toward the end of the world as they knew it, under the domination of the cruel Roman occupying forces, was then under way. The Messiah, their kingly leader, was about to appear at any moment to direct events and tell them what to do.

Although the message was simple, the impact it made was considerable. The Baptist was able to offer a straightforward yet moving baptism making people feel that they were acceptable to God and part of the new age. It was an alternative to the temple with its demands for dues or items for sacrifice. Even so it was only considered to be temporary, for when the new time came the Messiah would baptise with Holy Spirit and fire instead of water. Holy Spirit and fire are strong images and even today produce in us the feeling of awe.

> "I baptise you with water for repentance: but he who comes after me is mightier than I, whose shoes I am not worthy to hold: he shall baptise you with the Holy Spirit and with fire." Matthew 3:11

What happened next is told in John's gospel. A group of priests and Levites were sent by the temple leaders in Jerusalem to find out what John the Baptist was doing and saying. No doubt they were worried that someone could be undermining their position and even setting up some sort of rival organisation. The delegation travelled down to the River Jordan and asked him who he thought he was.

He quoted Isaiah saying that he is the voice of one crying in the wilderness:

> "Make straight the way of the Lord". John 1:23

WHY IN THE WILDERNESS?

Revolutions and armed uprisings started in the wilderness or desert where the troops would be assembled in secret ready to spring a surprise attack.

It was also a place of peace and solitude away from the evil ways of humans, and the Dead Sea Scrolls tell us that the Essenes thought that they would go into the wilderness at the final hour to separate themselves from evil people. To find God one retreated to a place of quiet as we still do today.

The wilderness was the natural place to think that God would want the forces of good to get ready for the battle against evil.

In other words he was the one telling the people to become pure and spiritually clean ready for the new age. We saw how the same idea occurred in the Dead Sea Scrolls and how the Essenes thought that they would be going into the wilderness to fight evil. The Baptist was not claiming anything more. He knew he was not the Messiah, but what he did believe was that the Messiah would be revealed at any moment. He told the delegation from Jerusalem:

> "In the midst of you stands one you do not know, even he that comes after me."   John 1:26-27

The Messiah was actually there amongst them but was unknown to them and, according to tradition, to the Messiah himself. The next day after the delegation had gone something happened. John the Baptist had a flash of realisation, an understanding, an insight, a vision. It was Jesus who was the Messiah.

> And he [John] looked upon Jesus as he walked, and said, "Behold, the Lamb of God"!   John 1:36

WHAT DOES 'THE LAMB OF GOD' MEAN?

'The Lamb of God' only appears in the gospels at this point. 'The Lamb' is used frequently in The Book of Revelation to symbolise the sacrifice of Jesus, but it is ill-suited here on the lips of the Baptist. He could not have known how Jesus was going to die nor understood the theology of the Crucifixion which was developed later.

There are two possibilities put forward by scholars. 1. The Baptist did not say it; the author wrote it into the story to stress to those reading the gospel that Jesus is the greater. 2. That the phrase could have well have been used by the Baptist; it was a way of talking about, without actually saying, the Messiah, and had links with the Old Testament.

So the Baptist revealed that it was Jesus who was the Messiah.

JESUS AND JOHN THE BAPTIST

JOHN THE BAPTIST	JESUS
PRIESTLY DESCENT. His father was a priest named Zechariah. (Luke 1:5) His mother Elizabeth was also of priestly descent. (Luke 1:6)	PRIESTLY FAMILY. Jesus came from a priestly background since he was related to John the Baptist through his mother Mary. (Luke 1:36)
PREPARING THE WAY. His role was to get people ready for the Messiah.	REVEALED AS THE MESSIAH. It was John the Baptist who first said that it was Jesus who was the Messiah.
SIMPLE LIFESTYLE. Lived in the wilderness feeding on wild foods.	LIVED IN THE WORLD. Jesus did not make fasting a rule for others. He lived to the full, mixing with all sorts.
PROPHET. Seen as a prophet baptising but did not heal.	PROPHET. Seen as a prophet and Messiah. Was a healer.
MISSION. To change the sinful, making them fit for the new age. Baptism was a symbol of a person's change.	MISSION. To bring as many as possible into close contact with God and into the new age no matter what they had done.
MURDERED. By king Herod who was fearful of the Baptist's ability to influence the population and cause an insurrection.	CRUCIFIED. His teaching was threatening the powerbase of those running the temple.

80

10 JESUS AND THE BAPTIST

The Gospel of John tells us nothing of the baptism of Jesus, not even that he was baptised by John the Baptist, although it does suggest it. We have to look to the synoptic account for that:-

> And it came to pass in those days, that Jesus, who came from Nazareth in Galilee, was baptised by John in the Jordan. And straightway coming up out of the water, he saw the heavens rent asunder and the Spirit as a dove descending upon him: and a voice came out of the heavens "Thou art my beloved Son." Mark 1:9-10

In ancient times the dove was a sign of the spirit. The role of the Baptist in the synoptic gospels was to baptise Jesus giving him the power from above. But in John's gospel the role of the Baptist was different; it was to reveal Jesus as the Messiah. The Baptist had a vision:

> 'I saw the Spirit descending as a dove out of heaven; like a dove and it rested on him.' John 1:32

He knew that Jesus was the Messiah. It was the turning point for both John the Baptist and Jesus; it was this vision which launched Jesus into his mission. Unfortunately life is not that simple. Jesus did not respond to the Baptist's proclamation. So next morning the Baptist told two of his own disciples.

> Again on the next day John was standing with two of his disciples and he looked at Jesus as he walked by and said, "Behold the Lamb of God!" And the two disciples heard him speak, and they followed Jesus.
>
> And Jesus turned and saw them following, and said to them, "What seek you?" And they said to him, "Rabbi" (which is to say, being interpreted, Teacher), "where are you staying?" He said unto them "Come, and you shall see". They came and saw where he was staying, and they stayed with him that day: it was about the tenth hour.
>
> One of the two who heard John speak and followed Jesus was Andrew, Simon Peter's brother. He finds first his own brother Simon, and said unto him, "We have found the Messiah" (which is, being interpreted, Christ). He brought Simon to Jesus. John 1:35-42

It was the two disciples who approached Jesus and attached themselves to him and not, as we are told in the dramatic synoptic account, Jesus who first called the disciples. The Gospel of John is not vague; the time of day was four in the afternoon and it was the next day that they left for Galilee. The story has the feeling of someone describing an event for which they had special memories and which happened some years previously.

Considering how and when Jesus recruited his disciples may seem a minor detail and not sufficiently important for us to worry about. But it is important because, if we take the account written by John as being correct, then Jesus and his followers were closely linked to the movement led by John the Baptist. We learn of this link in Acts in a speech made by Peter shortly after the Resurrection when a replacement for Judas was being chosen.

> Of the men therefore which have been our companions all the time that the Lord Jesus went in and out among us, beginning from the baptism of John, unto the day that he was received up from us, of these must one become a witness with us of his resurrection.
> Acts 1:21-22

It does not say that the disciples were followers of John the Baptist but the words 'beginning from the baptism of John' suggest that there was a connection between the two movements.

One might think that the disciples who left John the Baptist to join Jesus were deserting John. But it was not like that. Jesus and his followers were an offshoot of the Baptist movement, almost part of the same family, rather than being rivals.

To begin with, Jesus was following John the Baptist in his ideas and actions, but at the same time he does not seem to be entirely clear as to his exact role and future. At the wedding feast at Cana he told his mother:

> Mine hour is not yet come.   John 2:4

He was at the stage when he knew that change and something of importance was about to happen but, although living with the spirit, he did not yet know the exact form his ministry was to take. Most of us feel like this at some time in our lives.

After the wedding at Cana Jesus went to Capernaum for a short time, and then on to Jerusalem for the Passover, where the incident of cleansing the temple occurred. It has an Old Testament flavour and follows the preaching of John: that to be fit for the New Age there had to be a complete change in all ones actions as well as in spirit.

> And he found in the temple those that sold oxen and sheep and doves,

82

and the changers of money sitting: and he made a whip of cords and drove all out of the temple, both the sheep and the oxen; and he poured out the changers' money and overthrew their tables; and to them that sold the doves he said, "Take these things hence: make not my Father's house a house of merchandise".   John 2:14-16

In John's gospel the incident is at the start of the ministry. On the other hand in the synoptic accounts it occurs at the end just before the trial and Crucifixion. But if it was just before Jesus' death, surely the authorities would not have missed the opportunity to accuse Jesus at his trial of causing a disturbance in the temple? You can imagine how they would have made a central issue of it, but they did not. Having balanced all the evidence I have taken John's timing as the more likely with the incident happening at the start of Jesus' ministry.

Trying to alter the world by violently turning the money changers out of the temple is not in keeping with the non-violent message of Jesus in the rest of the New Testament. At the time he could have been, and probably was, frustrated at the way money played such an important part in the religious activity in the temple. He felt that he must take some action and do something about the way the people were behaving, attempting to get them to become pure in line with John's message.

But Jesus must have known in his heart that using force would not achieve much. Anyway the function of money changing was a very necessary part of financing the temple. The right amount of change was needed to buy a bird or an animal for sacrifice. So why did Jesus carry out this violent act?

A possible answer is that it was exactly what John the Baptist would have expected of him. There is a prophecy in the Old Testament (Malachi 3:1-4) which states that God will send a messenger —that is a prophet or Messiah— to prepare the way before him and purify the temple.

And he shall sit as a refiner and purifier of silver, and he shall purify the sons of Levi (the priests), and purge them as gold and silver; and they shall offer unto the Lord offerings in righteousness. Then shall the offering of Judah and Jerusalem be pleasant unto the LORD, as in the days of old, and as in ancient years.   Malachi 3:3-4

Jesus was demonstrating the need to purify the whole temple system, not just the money changers. The incident as told by John fits well at the start of Jesus' ministry.

83

We have seen how the synoptic gospels and the Gospel of John tell a different story of the events. Here is a summary of the differences during the first few months.

EVENT SEQUENCE AS SHOWN BY
THE SYNOPTIC AND JOHANNINE ACCOUNTS

IN THE SYNOPTIC ACCOUNTS

1. Jesus is baptised by John the Baptist.
2. The heavens open, a dove alights and a voice speaks.
3. Jesus departs into the wilderness and is tempted.
4. John the Baptist is killed by King Herod.
5. Jesus starts his ministry and calls the disciples.
6. At the very end of his life just before his trial Jesus expels the money changers from the temple.

IN THE JOHANNINE ACCOUNT

1. John the Baptist has a vision of a dove descending on Jesus.
2. He proclaims Jesus is the Messiah.
3. As nobody grasps the significance the Baptist repeats his revelation next day to two of his disciples.
4. The disciples claim Jesus to be the Messiah and bring in Peter.
5. Jesus and disciples leave for Galilee.
6. Not long after, during Passover, Jesus expels the money changers from the temple.

There are other instances of Jesus initially following John the Baptist's ideas. At the start of his ministry Jesus was baptising:

> After these things came Jesus and his disciples into Judaea, and he stayed there with them, and baptised.   John 3:22

Then later we read he was not baptising:

> When therefore the Lord knew how that the Pharisees had heard that Jesus was making and baptising more disciples than John (although Jesus himself baptised not, but his disciples) ...
> John 4:1-2

Later still neither Jesus nor his disciples were baptising. He was following his own course.

The incident of the fig-tree is another example of the Baptist's

84

teaching that those not living fruitful lives will be condemned.

> He hungered, and seeing a fig-tree some way off having leaves, he came, in case he would find anything on it: and when he came to it, he found nothing but leaves; for it was not the season of figs. He said to it, "No one shall eat fruit from you henceforward for ever".
>
> Mark 11:12-14

At first sight the story seems strange. It was most unjust for Jesus to condemn the fig-tree when it was not the time of year for figs. But the incident could have happened just before the cleansing of the temple in the early stages of his ministry. It must have been early spring for the tree to be in leaf but without edible fruit. Jesus had recently been revealed as the Messiah and it was believed that the new age was starting at that very time. The act was a symbol; it was saying to the people and the Jewish nation 'It is no good thinking you can put off changing your life until the new age starts. It has started and you must act now or be condemned forever.'

Then the crisis came. John the Baptist was put into prison by Herod and many people turned to Jesus as their leader.

Some saw him as a rebel chief who would be their national king and warrior leading them into battle against the Romans and winning victories against all odds. They knew it was possible, for had not Judas Maccabeus won a stunning victory against the large Syrian occupying forces almost 200 years before? Was not God on their side?

Others, such as the Essenes and followers of John the Baptist, saw the Messiah as sent by God to do away with the ungodly in some form of mystical war and bring in the new age. He would be a sort of religious superman on earth. During his time the debased temple system, making money out of the ordinary person and enriching the priests, would be replaced by a new order.

Jesus had to decide what to do. The pressure on him was great, for not only was he now more popular than John the Baptist, but he was singled out as the Messiah. There were a number of courses he could take. Should he become their rebel king, giving him a brief spell of power, but plunge the country into bloody conflict? Should he take the easy way and just concentrate on healing, which was popular, but which would be to neglect God's intention? Or should he go the way that he must have known as right; preaching and directing people spiritually for the Kingdom? It meant being blunt about the reform of the temple system, and would be sure to upset those running the temple. He would face certain death if God did not intervene in starting the new age, but he was in God's hands.

This crisis or temptation is recorded in the synoptic gospels. They tells us that Jesus withdrew into the wilderness to think things through. He had to come to a clear decision.

> And straightway the Spirit driveth him into the wilderness. And he was in the wilderness forty days tempted by Satan; and he was among the wild beasts; and the angels ministered unto him.
>
> Mark 1:12-13

The temptation is not recorded in John although there is about a month's space in the time sequence at this point.

Jesus was being carried forward by the Spirit. He had to teach that the search for the Kingdom of God, and how one finds it, is not what many people thought. His real work was about to start.

THE POOR

The poor were not those who were living off the land in poor economic circumstances. They were those who had suffered misfortune; e.g. the ill, the hungry, the blind, those who mourned, were in prison or in debt.

---

11 TO GALILEE AND THE KINGDOM

In the previous chapters we saw how John the Baptist was a powerful preacher. 'Repent, the kingdom of heaven is at hand' was his message. The time of the new era, or kingdom, was something to be feared, as only the good would survive into that second creation.

> And every tree that does not bring forth good fruit is cut down, and cast into the fire.   Luke 3:9

We saw how it was John the Baptist who singled out Jesus as the Messiah to lead those worthy into the golden age where there would be no evil. How Jesus started his ministry by taking on the Baptist's ideas, but during the first few months the emphasis of the ministry changed.

Jesus knew his task was to bring as many people as possible into that kingdom. It was not only those who had been through baptism or temple rituals to make them 'clean' and worthy that were acceptable, but anyone who had a close relationship with God. Jesus wasn't preaching another message in opposition to John the Baptist; his teaching was following on from the Baptist.

In the Gospel of John, we are told that Jesus was very successful during the early part of his ministry. So much so that he left to go to Galilee so that he would not be competing with John the Baptist for followers.

> He left Judaea and departed again for Galilee. He had to pass through Samaria ...   John 4:3-4

It was now summer and hot, very hot and dusty, and especially down in the Jordan valley. So hot that he chose not to use the route through the valley. Instead he followed the higher cooler road along the top of the hills, through the country of Samaria.

It was here that he met the Samaritan woman by Jacob's well. The story is enchanting as it summarises all of Jesus' teaching and is when his ministry really starts. When reading it in chapter 4 of John's gospel remember, as explained previously, the gospel is like a play written by one person with the purpose of drawing out in depth what Jesus was saying.

By asking this woman for a drink Jesus was breaking many of the rules of his time. He was talking to a woman on his own, a thing frowned upon. As she was a not a Jew he should not be using her drinking cup, because it would not be ritually clean. Furthermore, she had 'five husbands', which made it all very much worse.

Why was she at Jacob's Well some way from the village and on her own? Probably because she was of low repute and would have been prevented by the villagers from using the village well. They would have thought that her ritual uncleanliness might contaminate their water or pots used for carrying water. Jesus was befriending this outcast because the coming age was for all, provided, that is, they followed Jesus' message:-

> Jesus answered and said to her "Everyone that drinks this water shall thirst again: but whoever drinks of the water that I shall give him shall never thirst; but the water that I shall give him shall become in him a well of water springing up unto eternal life."
>
> John 4:13-14

The conversation continues with the Samaritan woman saying that Jesus, a Jew, would say that they, the Samaritans, should worship in the temple in Jerusalem, rather than in their own temple. Their temple was near to where they were standing on mount Gerizim. The reply Jesus made is interesting:-

> Jesus said to her, "Woman, believe me, the hour is coming when neither on this mountain, nor in Jerusalem, shall you worship the Father. ... But the hour is coming, and now is, when the true worshippers shall worship the Father in spirit and truth: for such does the Father want of

In other words the kingdom, or new creation, had started and the temple worship as it then was, with animal sacrifices to appease God, would be replaced by something different. This would have been popular with the poor peasants who neither had the time, nor the money, to go to the temple. But it was absolutely unacceptable to the Jews who ran the temple in Jerusalem.

Jesus' prophesy of the destruction is told in both John's gospel and in the synoptic accounts. After saying "There shall not be left here one stone upon another" he continues:–

> "And you shall hear of wars and rumours of wars, be not troubled: these things must come to pass; but the end is not yet. For nation shall rise against nation, and kingdom against kingdom: and there shall be famines and earthquakes in many places. But all these things are the beginning of labour."   Mark 13:7–8

If you read on then you will see that the golden age was to be born out of violence and supernatural happenings:–

> But in those days, after that ordeal, the sun shall be darkened, and the moon shall not give her light; and the stars shall be falling from heaven, and the powers that are in the heavens shall be shaken. And then shall they see the Son of man coming in clouds with great power and glory.
> Mark 13:24

The temple would be destroyed by these supernatural powers and rebuilt by Jesus in his new state:–

> The Jews answered and said to him, "What sign can you show us proving that you can do these things?" Jesus answered and said to them "Destroy this temple, and in three days I will raise it up."
> John 2:18-19

Jesus saw that, in some way, he would be part of these other-worldly happenings. You will remember that the Essenes thought of the end very much in the same terms, so there was nothing new in these ideas. But Jesus did not just tell of the kingdom as a coming of the new age; it took many forms. For instance it could be thought of as here and now.

Returning to the story of the woman of Samaria and the events at that time, we learn that Jesus stayed in the village for two days and that many Samaritans came to believe in him. We sometimes forget that Jesus must have had quite a following in the foreign country of Samaria. We are told in Acts of the Apostles that the disciples Philip, Peter and John (Zebedee) were successfully working in the area just after the death of Jesus.

Jesus spent the next year teaching and healing in Galilee. It was the high point in his ministry, and the story of the paralysed man being let down through the roof of a house because the crowd of people prevented the man from entering (Mark 2:1-5) gives a vivid picture of Jesus' popularity. In October, as would be expected of a holy man, he made a visit to Jerusalem for the festival of The Tabernacles. As we saw on page 28, every Jew was supposed to take part in the three main religious festivals at the temple; The Passover, The Dedication and The Tabernacles, and this was what Jesus was doing.

Back in Galilee, Jesus continued his work as healer and prophet. Then, some time at the beginning of the year, John the Baptist was murdered by Herod.

12 PROCLAIM HIM KING

You will know the gruesome story of the murder of John the Baptist recorded in Matthew and Mark. How Herod had wrongly married his brother's wife, and was condemned by the Baptist. How the daughter of Herod's wife danced before him, and how he was so pleased that he promised anything only to be asked for the head of the Baptist on a plate.

You may wonder why this nasty murder tale is in the New Testament. But John the Baptist was seen at the time, and by the early church, as an important part of the happenings leading up to the end of time and the new creation. As the person to have announced the start of it all, the one who had revealed who was the Messiah, this true prophet had given a 'seal of approval' to the fact that Jesus was indeed the Messiah.

What effect did the murder have on Jesus? It increased the expectation of the followers of both men that the new era was close. To understand their feelings we need to go back and follow the course of events. John the Baptist had a large following, and he and his disciples were looking to Jesus as the Messiah. The Baptist was imprisoned, and like anyone else in prison, had plenty of time to think and have doubts.

> Now when John who was in the prison heard the works of the Christ, he sent by his disciples a message: "Are you he that is to come, or should we look for another?" And Jesus answered and said to them, "Go back and tell John the things which you do hear and see: the blind receive their sight, and the lame walk, the lepers are cleansed, and the deaf hear, and the dead are raised up, the poor have good tidings preached to them".
>
> Matthew 11:2-5

Jesus' reply was not a direct 'Yes'. That would have been easy to say but would not have been convincing. Telling them to look at what was happening, and asking them to draw their own conclusions, was so much better.

So they went back to John the Baptist excited about the big event that they thought was to happen shortly. Later, when the murder of the Baptist happened they must have felt that it was another signal that history was moving forward.

In March or April, when Jesus had been in Galilee teaching and

91

healing for almost a year, we come to the feeding of the five thousand. This popular name for the story is confusing since there are two figures given in the New Testament for the number of people fed; 5,000 and 4,000. Luke and John both give only the larger figure, but Matthew and Mark quote the larger and smaller numbers. We do not know if these were two separate incidents with different numbers of people, or only one with two slightly different accounts. Most scholars think that it was the same incident which has come down from two different sources.

Jesus went up onto a hillside where a large crowd came to find him.

> One of his disciples, Andrew, Simon Peter's brother, said to him, "There is a lad here, who has five barley loaves and two fishes: but what are these among so many?" Jesus said, "Make the people sit down". Now there was much grass in the place, so the men sat down, in number about five thousand. Jesus then took the loaves; and having given thanks he distributed to those that sat there: likewise also with the fishes, as much as they needed. John 6:8-11

The original Greek text in the parallel passage in Mark clearly refers to the crowd as men. John then goes on to tell us:-

> When the people saw the sign Jesus did, they said, "In truth this is the prophet that is to come into the world". Jesus perceiving that they were about to come and forcibly make him king, withdrew again into the mountains by himself. John 6:14-15

The king that they wanted was an earthly king. A king who would govern them and make the nation strong by massacring their enemies. He would be like King David who, almost a thousand years beforehand, had forged an independent nation.

The Galileans were quarrelsome, staunch nationalists and difficult to get on with. They were relatively wealthy so they could afford to be aggressive. Josephus tells us:-

> For the Galileans are hardened to war from their infancy, and have been always very numerous; nor has the country ever lacked men of courage, or been in want of them; for their soil is universally rich and fruitful, and full of the plantations of trees of all sorts, ... it is all cultivated by its inhabitants, and no part of it lies idle.
> Josephus, Jewish War

The kingdom was to be won by fighting, by a rebellion, as in the days of the Maccabees, with God on their side. Uprisings started by gatherings in the desert, and it is likely this crowd of men on the hill side were hoping that Jesus would lead them in battle. This certainly was not what Jesus had in mind! So, to cool down the passions of the crowd, he withdrew by himself, and later (as recorded in Mark 8:27–38) had to make it plain to his disciples that the kingdom was not to be found in this way.

Instead of going to Jerusalem for the Passover and being drawn into the wrong sort of conflict, he took evasive action by leaving Galilee and travelling into Gentile territory. We learn from the synoptic account that he wanted to get away and did not want people to know where he was.

> And from there he arose, and went away into the regions of Tyre and Sidon. And he entered into a house, and would have no man know it: but he could not hide. But straightaway a woman whose little daughter had an unclean spirit, having heard about him, came and fell at his feet. Now the woman was a Gentile, a Phoenician of Syria by race.
>
> Mark 7:24-25

Then follows the story of how, after Jesus said she was not a Jew, she got him to cure her daughter by telling him that even the dogs under the table could eat the children's scraps.

From now on Jesus was constantly preparing his disciples for the climax of his life, the dawn of the golden age, and his death in Jerusalem.

> However, I must be on my way to-day and to-morrow and the day after: for it cannot be that a prophet dies outside Jerusalem.
>
> O Jerusalem, Jerusalem, which kills the prophets, and stones them that are sent to her! How often would I have gathered your children together, even as a hen gathers her own brood under her wings, but you would not allow me! Behold, your temple is left for you desolate: and I say to you, you shall not see me until you will say, "Blessed is he that comes in the name of the Lord."
>
> Luke 13:33-35

It would have been sometime around September that Jesus left Galilee and headed for Jerusalem for the last time. It was autumn and, like the previous year, he was going for the festival of the Tabernacles. This time he did not go publicly but 'almost in secret', as he knew the dangers which could face him there.

At some risk he taught in the temple.

> Therefore some of the people of Jerusalem said, "Is this not he whom they seek to kill? And look, he speaks openly, and they say nothing to

him. Can it be that the rulers indeed know that this is the Christ?"
John 7:25-26

The rulers were those who ran the temple. John calls them the chief priests and Pharisees and, although the chief priests (the Sadducees) were the ones in charge, the Pharisees were also involved. It was these rulers who sent the temple police to arrest Jesus.

> The officers therefore came to the chief priests and Pharisees; and they said to them, "Why did you not bring him?" The officers answered, "Never a man spoke as this man." John 7:45-46

So the impact of the words of Jesus saved him from being arrested. For the next month he and his disciples were probably travelling in Judaea with the disciples being sent out to cover as many villages as possible.

> And as they went on the road, a certain man said to him, "I will follow you wherever you go." And Jesus said to him, "The foxes have holes, and the birds of the heaven have nests; but the Son of man has nowhere to lay his head". Luke 9:57-58

In December Jesus once again went to the temple, this time for the festival of Dedication. Once more an attempt was made to arrest him, but he avoided being captured. He retreated to Bethany-beyond-Jordan on the other side of the river Jordan, to the warm river valley where John the Baptist had been baptising two years beforehand.

We are not told how Jesus managed to slip away from the temple police; maybe he was warned that they were about to arrest him. He, as well as his disciples, certainly knew that the end was not far away especially if he did return to Jerusalem again.

We then read in chapter 11 of the gospel how he got an urgent message to go to Lazarus. The disciples worried that he would be killed.

The sisters Martha and Mary lived in the other village called Bethany just two miles from Jerusalem. They sent a plea to Jesus to come quickly to help their brother, Lazarus, who was ill.

> When therefore he [Jesus] heard that he [Lazarus] was sick, he stayed for two days in the place where he was. Then after this he said to the disciples, "Let us go into Judaea again." The disciples said to him "Rabbi,

the Jews were wanting to stone you; and go you there again?"

John 11:6-8

After further conversation:

Thomas therefore, who is called the 'Twin', said to his fellow-disciples, "Let us also go, that we may die with him."

John 11:16

Everyone in the group knew that the future was uncertain. Why did Jesus wait two days before deciding to go up the steep mountain road back to Judaea? Perhaps because he was hoping for a further message to say that he was not needed, but we can only guess. Jesus was now at that point where, if he answered the call, the end would not be far off. But he had to go to save Lazarus.

GOD DOES NOT DO THINGS FOR US

It may seem surprising but the fact is that the gospels do not tell us that God will do things for us. They make it quite clear that God gives us the power to do things ourselves. Here are the passages about asking and being given, starting with John's Gospel which is quoted most often. I have put in italics the important parts.

> Verily, verily, I say unto you, He that believeth on me, the works that I do *shall he do also*; and greater works than these *shall he do*; because I go unto the Father. And whatsoever you shall ask in my name that I will do, that the Father may be glorified in the Son. If you shall ask me anything in my name, that will I do.
>
> John 14:12-14

The writing is ambiguous, it is possible to read it in two ways. (As with many of the writings in the Bible). It could mean that you ask for something and it is done for you. Or it could also mean that you will be given the power to do the thing yourself. The whole passage must be taken together and the first sentence must be linked to the second. The second cannot be taken in isolation. When read as one it makes it clear that *you* are being given the power to do things. It does not say that you can sit back letting God do the work like some genie in a bottle. John repeats the idea in his gospel.

> Ask whatsoever you will, and it shall be done *unto you*.
>
> John 15:7

> I chose you and appointed you, that you should go and bear fruit and that your fruit should live: that whatever you shall ask of the Father in my name he may *give it to you*.   John 15:16

> If you shall ask anything of the Father, he will give it *to you* in my name.   John 16:23

> So far you have asked nothing in my name: ask, and *you shall receive*.   John 16:24

This view is also supported by the synoptic gospels.

> And all things, whatsoever you shall ask in prayer, believing, *you* shall receive.   Matt. 21:22

> Ask and it shall be given *to you*; seek, and *you* shall find; knock, and it shall be opened *unto you*.   Matt. 7:7

There are also two more passages in Mark (11:24) and Luke (11:9) but as they say exactly the same thing they are not repeated.

The gospels are telling us that by receiving this power, the Holy Spirit or whatever you like to call it, we are enabled to go forward in strength.

13 THE LAST MONTH

'You shall have no other gods before me.'   Exodus 20:3

The commandment that there be only one god worshipped is central to the Jewish faith now, and always was so. To worship another god was unthinkable, and we saw in chapter 4 how the introduction of Greek gods by the Syrians at the time of the Maccabees sparked off a revolt. Many people then, and later, chose to die rather than accept other gods.

Yet, at the time of Jesus, the world was seen to be alive with demons and spirits both good and bad. Everything —animals, crops and the weather— was influenced by these powers which were being used by God to control the world.

Ill health, especially mental illness, was thought to be caused by demons. And these demons were sent by God to lodge in the person as a consequence of some sin which had been committed. If a cure was wanted, the first step was to repent of the sin, even if one did not know what it was. It meant going to a priest and making an offering at the temple, and only after that could what we call medicine be used to make a cure. Had medicine been used straight away, that would have been a sign that the sick person did not have faith in God.

In the case of madness the evil spirit or demon residing in the body could be exorcised, commanded to leave, by a holy man using God's power through prayer. Jesus cast out these unclean spirits. The story of the man living amongst the tombs, breaking his iron fetters and chains, is told in Mark 5:1-20. First Jesus asked the spirit its name, because if you knew the name of a demon you had power over it. Then Jesus commanded it to go. It left, and went into a herd of pigs which rushed into the water and the pigs drowned.

The disciples were given the power to heal:

> And he called to him his twelve disciples, and gave them authority over unclean spirits, to cast them out and to heal all manner of disease and all manner of sickness.   Matthew 10:1

They were not the only ones healing at that time, for there are many references to healers at work. The Essenes were healers and

97

there is mention in the gospels of others healing. When Jesus' opponents were accusing him of using black magic he replied that he could not be doing it in the name of Beelzebub the prince of devils, as good came from his healings. He goes on:

"And if I by Beelzebub cast out devils, by whom do your own followers cast them out? Therefore shall they be your judges."
Matthew 12:27

These other healers were also doing it through prayer, but there were crooks as well. As now, there are genuine faith healers who work using prayer and the power of God, and there are some con men and women who pretend to have that power to push themselves forward, or to get money. Simon Magus was one of these and

used sorcery, and amazed the people of Samaria, giving out that himself was some great one. Acts 8:9

He tried to buy the power of the Holy Spirit from Peter, but was quickly told to repent and pray the Lord he would be forgiven. Jesus got nothing from his healing; he just healed from compassion and love of humanity. Often he told those whom he had healed not to tell anyone. Much the same happened with his miracles.

The very word miracle immediately makes us sit up and give our strong views about them. Some think miracles are just nonsense and are easily explained by science. Others, that God does things which are normally impossible. We get worked up about it all, and it spoils our reading of the Bible.

We have been brought up to think and analyse in a scientific way. When anything happens we automatically try to fathom out the cause. If we are sick, we think of the different foods we have eaten. If there are unusual storms or a drought we wonder if it is the earth heating up because of the greenhouse effect. If someone appears to be walking on water, we at once ask ourselves 'How is it done?' Are there shallows to account for it? What are the explanations? We try to be detectives, like Sherlock Holmes, finding the reasons for everything.

In the past it was not like that. It was God who made everything work. That did not mean to say that there was no feeling for cause and effect. If you put your hand in the fire it would burn! But if Jesus appeared to be walking on water there would be no debate as to whether he really did. There would be no looking for some scientific reason to account for it; it would just be a sign from God that he looked as if he was.

So let it be with us today. Let us recognise that the power of prayer is immense, and miracles such as healings do occur whether or not a scientific explanation can be found. How we view the miracles should not make a difference to our faith. It was not an issue in New Testament times, so why get hot under the collar about it now? Surely we can look at the evidence around a happening and just let it rest there without trying to prove how God is acting.

Jesus was under pressure to use his miracle making skills to get people to believe in him. But he was reluctant.

> Therefore they said to him, "What can you do to give us a sign, that we may see, and so believe in you?" John 6:30

He told them that he would not provide food as Moses had done in the desert, the miracle described in Exodus 16:31. Instead he would give them spiritual bread. He was not going to become a magician. All the same, the crowds following Jesus saw that his healings and miracles were from God; they were a sign that he was a prophet —someone speaking on behalf of God.

Bringing back to life from the dead was thought to be a major sign from God. Elijah, one of the greatest of prophets, brought back to life the son of a poor widow, and in Acts we are told about it happening in the early church. Jesus, as well as healing, brought three people back to life.

You will see from this table that the three people Jesus brought back to life are not reported in all the gospels.

PERSON FROM DEAD	BY	WHERE IN BIBLE
Poor Widow's son	Elijah,	1 Kings 17:17
Daughter of Jairus.	Jesus	Matt 9:23; Mark 5:23; Luke 8:43
Widow's son at Nain.	Jesus	Luke 7:11–17
Lazarus at Bethany.	Jesus	John 11:38–44
Dorcas at Joppa	Peter	Acts 9:40
Eutychus at Troas	Paul	Acts 20:9–12

The raising of Lazarus is only recorded in John. There is something strange about the story.

First of all why did Jesus after hearing that Lazarus was sick wait two days and then say that Lazarus was asleep followed by the statement that he was dead? This is what John says:-

> "Our friend Lazarus has fallen asleep; but I go that I may awake him out of sleep". The disciples therefore said to him, "Lord, if he has fallen asleep he will recover." Now Jesus had spoken of his death: but they thought that he spoke of resting sleep. Then Jesus said to them plainly: "Lazarus is dead."   John 11:11-14

Secondly, why did this act of bringing back to life cause so much opposition that both Jesus and Lazarus were condemned by the Jewish council soon afterwards? To be condemned after being brought back to life is strange.

You can chose between these four suggestions as to what happened and modify them as you see fit.

1. The story as told by John is as it happened with Jesus working a miracle of raising the dead.

2. The episode was a result of creative writing by John in order make his points. It has theological significance. e.g. Lazarus: death plus two days equals life; Jesus: Crucifixion plus two days equals Resurrection.

3. An old manuscript was found which referred to a letter (which could be a fake) from Clement of Alexandria who died in AD 214. This letter quoted a secret part of the Gospel of Mark. It told that Jesus when at Bethany raised a rich young man from a tomb. Then six days later Jesus taught him the mystery of the kingdom of God. The theory is that it was an initiation or baptism rite likened to the old Egyptian gods who were thought to descend into darkness and come out new.

4. Lazarus, with others or on his own accord, put himself into a trance. He could have been trying to get 'a trip' for a religious experience, attempting some religious initiation rite or just hoping in some way to become a disciple of Jesus.

Nowadays many men and women go into trances, and you will have seen examples on TV in the programmes about religious sects or primitive peoples. It has happened throughout the ages and there are examples in the New Testament. We read in Acts that both Peter and Paul went into trances. Peter had a vision whilst praying in the town of Joppa and Paul in the Jerusalem temple also whilst praying.

At the time Lazarus went into the tomb Jesus was by the River Jordan so he could not have been involved. He must have known what was going on and hence his saying that Lazarus was asleep yet dead. So he could take his time to go to Lazarus.

The reason why the incident caused so much opposition from the authorities could have been that it was not a straightforward raising from the dead. Although we do not know what happened it would not have worried Jesus. He was always more concerned about a relationship with God than a religious action.

Immediately afterwards those who controlled the temple acted. They called a meeting of the Sanhedrin, the political council which ruled under the Romans, and the council agreed that Jesus must die. It had not the power to execute a prisoner. That had to be done with the agreement of, and by, the Romans. A warrant for Jesus' arrest was issued, probably with a reward. So he went into hiding, a wanted man.

So from that day on they schemed how they might put him to death. Jesus therefore did not go about openly among the Jews, but departed for the country-side on the edge of the desert, to a village called Ephraim; and there he stayed with the disciples.

John 11:53-54

Now the chief priests and the Pharisees had given orders, that, if any person knew where he was, they should say, so that they might arrest him.

John 11:57

It is not known where Ephraim was, but it is thought that it was in a small isolated fertile valley not far from the present town of Ramallah, only 10 miles north of Jerusalem. There are caves for shelter, a water supply, and the woods with spring flowers would have made it a most peaceful spot for Jesus and the disciples.

I was at Ramallah in the spring just before Easter and was at a church service. It was at the same time of year that Jesus was there, and during the service we were reminded of how he must have felt, in hiding, just two miles down the road. It was a most moving experience.

Jesus was hiding here, probably for a month or more, before returning to the home of Mary, Martha and Lazarus in Bethany. He had come for the Passover, to be at the temple for the festival

101

with all the thousands of milling pilgrims.

A Jew would not have travelled on the Sabbath as that was considered to be work, so Jesus journeyed on our Sunday, six days before the next Sabbath. This table sets out what happened on which days during the final week.

DAY	WHAT JESUS WAS DOING
Saturday (Sabbath)	At Ephraim in hiding. (John 11:54)
Sunday	Travels to Bethany. Supper and anointing. (John 12:1-8)
Monday	Palm 'Sunday', the triumphal entry. (John 12:12-19)
Tuesday	Jesus in hiding. (John 12:36)
Wednesday	Jesus in hiding. (John 12:36)
Thursday	Last supper. Night arrest. (John 13:2, 18:1-27)
Friday	Trial, crucifixion and burial. (John 18:28-19:42)
Saturday (Sabbath)	Passover.
Sunday	Empty tomb very early in morning.(John 20:1-18)

You will see that Jesus entered Jerusalem on Monday morning after his stay in Bethany. We can all visualise the scene with Jesus riding on a donkey, the people laying down palm branches in front of him and shouting 'God bless the King of Israel'. A warrior king would have ridden a horse, but he sat on the donkey to show that his was the religious kingdom. He was not going to start an uprising.

At the last supper Jesus washed the disciples' feet.

Jesus, knowing that the Father had entrusted all things into his hands, and that he came from God, and was going to God, rose from the supper table, and laid aside his garments; and he took a towel, and tied it round himself. Then he poured water into the basin, and began to wash the disciples' feet, and to wipe them with the towel withwhich he had around himself. John 13:3-5

In hot dusty countries the washing of feet is most refreshing. Certainly the master or mistress of a household would never have washed the feet of their servants. Why did Jesus do it? He says:

"You call me 'Teacher' and 'Lord': and it is well said for so I am. If I

102

then, the Lord and Teacher, have washed your feet, you also ought to wash one another's feet. For I have set you an example: that you also should do as I have done to you. Verily, verily, I say unto you, a servant is not greater than his lord; neither is the one that is sent greater than the person that sent him. If you know these things, blessed are you if you do them." John 13:13-17

The act of washing the disciples feet was symbolic. It was a demonstration or symbol of how one should think and behave. You have a duty to 'wash the feet' of the people who are less fortunate than yourself.

Jesus did things in a symbolic way to explain his message. His miracles were a demonstration of God's love. He rode into Jerusalem on a donkey to show that he was not a military king. Twelve Apostles were chosen to symbolise the twelve tribes of Israel coming together at the start of the kingdom. Even the last supper itself had deep meanings. To share a meal with others is to make a bond of friendship, and Jesus knew that this was the last meal before he would go and before the new and wonderful age would start.

Jesus knowing that his hour was come, that he should depart out of this world to the Father. John 13:1

"Verily I say to you, I will no more drink of the fruit of the vine, until that day when I drink it new in the kingdom of God." Mark 14:25

In the new kingdom, with no bad feelings or squabbles, there would be a deep fellowship between everyone. Jesus was using the close bond that existed between the disciples around the table to show what it would be like. As we have just seen he said 'If you know these things, blessed are you if you do them.'

Then something unexpected happens.

Jesus was troubled in the spirit, and proclaimed saying, "Verily, verily, I say to you, that one of you shall betray me" John 13:21

Jesus gives some bread to Judas Iscariot, and goes on to tell him:

"What you do, do quickly." Now no one at the table knew why he spoke this to him. John 13:27-28

Immediately Judas goes out to tell the temple authorities where Jesus will be found later that night.

103

An arrest can be made in darkness with no crowds of watching pilgrims to object. So Judas was given a signal by Jesus to go and betray him. We are not told why and we can only make guesses. But first we need to look at what happened next day.

14 KINGDOM NOT OF THIS WORLD

The week before Easter, Holy Week, always makes me uncomfortable. To pore over the arrest, trial and nasty death of Jesus is certainly no pleasure. It is just one more of those tragedies which the newspapers seem to love, and of which we have too much.

The writer of John's gospel could have had much the same feelings because how he describes things changes. From the time of Jesus' arrest (at the start of chapter 18) to the end of the gospel he tells us what happened in a straightforward way not dwelling over the details. He drops Jesus' long speeches which have done their job explaining the message, and just allows the rest of the story to speak for itself.

There is no point in repeating everything that happened during that last night and the following day. It is better that you read the account yourself. But there are some things which are not normally included in the bible commentaries because commentaries do not always take John's gospel as being as reliable historically as the synoptic gospels.

The temple police, guided by Judas Iscariot, came at night to arrest Jesus. The Jewish police did not use weapons such as swords, but kept the crowds in order with their dreaded truncheons. On this occasion, in case there was any difficulty with the troublesome Galileans who were prone to insurrections, they were accompanied by a squad of Roman soldiers. The Jewish leaders who ran the temple had to involve the fully armed Romans even though to collaborate with the occupying force would have antagonised the Jewish people.

Jesus, instead of resisting or escaping to fight at another time as would be expected with a rebel leader, made himself known to those who came to get him. At this point the gospel says that the soldiers stepped back and fell down. Although this reflects the original Greek it is probably a misunderstanding. What was meant was that the soldiers stepped back and lowered their weapons, or dropped their guard as is said in some sports such as boxing. When they realised that they were not going to be attacked they felt that they could relax.

Why did the Roman soldiers leave it to the temple police to take Jesus for questioning by the high priests? Surely, at the slightest hint of trouble the Romans would have dealt with it themselves.

There were two reasons. Firstly, Jesus had been condemned by the Jewish court and the matter was still a Jewish affair. Secondly, it is unlikely that the Roman soldiers saw Jesus as someone who would be causing an uprising. The keeping of the peace in that turbulent land was the army's main concern and the small number of disciples was no major threat. Indeed, none of the followers were taken by the soldiers, as they would have been if there had been any risk of rebellion against the ruthless Roman rulers.

Jesus had already been condemned by the Sanhedrin a month beforehand, but it was the Jewish law that the accused should be heard in person. With Jesus in custody the legal formalities were quickly completed.

Jesus had done nothing which could allow the Sadducees who held power to execute him and so get rid of him. He had not blasphemed by saying that he was God. True, he had done many things which were deeply offensive to many of the Jewish leaders. He had shown solidarity with the worst people by sharing meals with them, but that was not a crime. He had criticised the temple authorities, but that was not a religious crime. He had said the most dreadful things, such as "Let the dead bury the dead". To neglect responsibility toward the dead was unthinkable and one of the worst things one could do, but not a crime calling for death.

His real crime, then again not punishable by death, was to attack those who ran the temple, thus undermining their authority. For this he had to be silenced. It was to Pilate, the Roman governor, that they took him on trumped-up charges.

The trial before Pilate is given in some detail in John's gospel. Jesus makes it quite clear that he is not a rebel and is not concerned with worldly things. He tells Pilate

"My kingdom is not of this world: If my kingdom were of this world, then would my servants fight that I should not be arrested by the Jews: but my kingdom is not like that."   John 18:36

It comes through that Pilate was doing all that he could not to condemn Jesus. He even tried to appeal to the crowd over the heads of the accusers to allow him to release Jesus. But no, it was Barabbas a Zealot who had started an uprising whom they wanted to go free. There was no alternative when the Jewish powers threatened menacingly:

"If you release this man, you are not Caesar's friend."
John 19:12

If the word had got to Rome that he was a 'softie', not keeping the nation under strict control, or in any way disloyal to the Emperor, he could easily have lost favour in Rome and his position. So Jesus was handed over to the army for crucifixion.

Busy rulers such as Pilate did not spend much time on what to them were fairly minor affairs. Life was cheap and the lives of those who were not Roman citizens were even more expendable. Sentences were harsh and with the ordinary person were passed without the worry we have today in most countries. Josephus the historian tells of two thousand ringleaders of an uprising being crucified by the Roman general Varus around the time of Jesus' birth. So why did Pilate go to such lengths to free Jesus? We do not know, but in Matthew there is a strange passage:

While Pilate was sitting on the judgement-seat, his wife sent a message to him saying, "Have nothing to do with that good man, for I have suffered many things last night in a dream because of him."
Matthew 27:19

Also, in Jewish writings not so long after the time of Jesus, there is a passage describing Jesus as being 'connected with the government'. We know that Jesus had many influential followers, such as Nicodemus and Joseph of Arimathea. So it is probable that he may have had followers in Pilate's household perhaps amongst the women. If this was so then we might have some ideas about the question we asked at the end of the last chapter. Why was Judas given a signal by Jesus to go out and betray him?

Many people have had different ideas and theories as to what happened during that final week two thousand years ago. Here are a two suggestions.

1. The Kingdom of God, the new era, was thought to be about to start at any moment. The life of the Messiah Jesus was moving to an end, and with the Passover festival his new role in the new order

was beginning. Judas may have felt that if he worked with God to bring about the new age it would happen faster. So bringing on a show-down with the authorities was a way of helping the new age to start. The idea that one works with God is common to most of us. Do we not do things for the church, or even fight battles to make a better world?

2. You will remember that Jesus was sentenced to death and was in hiding for about one month before the Passover. Judas could have been working to free Jesus from the sentence. He might have thought that the influence that Jesus' followers had in Pilate's household would have been sufficient to get him freed by Pilate. Certainly Judas did not expect him to be condemned to death.

Then Judas, which betrayed him, when he saw Jesus was condemned, repented himself, and brought back the thirty pieces of silver to the chief priests and elders, saying, "I have sinned in that I betrayed innocent blood." But they said, "What is that to us? see you to it." And he threw down the pieces of silver into the temple sanctuary and departed; and went away and hanged himself.   Matthew 27:3-5

Life is never straightforward and we do things for a number of reasons. So the truth could have been a bit of both the ideas suggested as well as other reasons which we know nothing about. It does not matter that we do not know exactly what happened, the important thing is to grasp the message of these last days. Jesus was doing what he knew was right, whatever the outcome.

Sometimes it is said that the disciples ran away frightened at the time of the Crucifixion. It was just the women who were left to comfort Jesus in his last hours. Certainly women played a much greater part in the formation of the new church than is understood at first sight in the New Testament.

That the disciples were not at the cross does not mean that they abandoned Jesus. The Roman soldiers, carrying out an execution of those convicted of causing trouble, would not have risked having supporters hanging around looking for a chance to rescue their leader. Only women and children would have been allowed anywhere nearby.

At the cross

When Jesus therefore saw his mother, and the disciple standing by, whom he loved, he said to his mother, "Woman, there is your son!" Then he said to the disciple, "There is your mother!" And from that hour the disciple took her into his own home.   John 19:26-27

We do not know who was 'the disciple whom he loved'. It is possible that he was the author of John's gospel. He must have been young to have been allowed to be so near to Jesus to talk to him, yet old enough and sufficiently wealthy to be able to take Mary back to his home.

Discipline in the Roman army was strict. If the soldiers who were ordered to carry out an execution did not do so, they would have been executed themselves. The temptation to accept a bribe and say that the prisoner was dead, when he was not, would have been great. So, as Jesus was not alive and to ensure that he really was dead, a spear was thrust into his side aiming for the heart.

... and at once there came out blood and water. And he that had seen it has told us about it, and his evidence is true.   John 19:34-35

This could have been one of the servants removing the body. It is unlikely to have been the youth as he had gone home with Mary.

It was late on the eve of the great festival of the Passover as well as the eve of the Sabbath, so ritual purity was all important for this double occasion. Nicodemus and Joseph of Arimathea, the two wealthy disciples, with the help of their servants rushed to bury the body of Jesus before nightfall. The feast started at nightfall and the handling of a dead body at that time would have excluded them from partaking. As there was not time to anoint and wash the body properly, they temporarily wrapped it with

...a mixture of myrrh and aloes, about 70 pounds in weight.
                                                        John 19:39

In that hot climate it would keep the body sweet-smelling until it could be attended to on the morning after the feast. That was on 'the third day', which was to change everything.

1st day	Friday afternoon late	– death and quick burial.
2nd day	Saturday	– Sabbath and Passover festival.
3rd day	Sunday very early	– The day of the Resurrection.

In the Creed it says:– "The third day he rose again from the dead". But it is confusing as he had been dead no more than one and a half days. Here the counting is inclusive, when the first and last days are included. We sometimes count like this. The holiday brochures can talk of a three-day holiday even when you start late on the first day, have one day on the beach, and leave early next morning.

What happened on that third day moves the story outside of the happenings of everyday life, bound by time and space. It moves into the realms of religious experience, the workings of God of which Jesus had been talking: things which can only be understood by experience and not by scientific logic. By studying what happened next, not only at the time but later in the lives of the followers of Jesus, we may get a glimpse of the truth. Perhaps we can even be at one with the spiritual power that comes to us across time from those ancient days.

DIFFERENCE BETWEEN DISCIPLE AND APOSTLE.

A disciple of Jesus is one who follows Jesus and learns from him. It could be anyone at any time in history, now or during the lifetime of Jesus.

An Apostle is one of the original followers of Jesus sent out by him as a messenger to preach the gospel. Paul called himself an apostle although he was not one of the original followers, because Jesus appeared to him at his conversion.

Jesus chose twelve apostles, probably one representing each of the twelve tribes. The twelve are not precisely named in the New Testament nor in other writings of the time. They suggest that Jesus may have been talking about the twelve in a symbolic way and may not have been too worried if there were a few more or less than exactly twelve. He was always more concerned with spiritual matters than exactness of the rule book so the suggestion is quite possible.

---

15 "I HAVE SEEN HIM"

Let us imagine the scene during the final week-end as recorded by John.

April has just started and the green countryside outside Jerusalem is flecked with bright colours of wild flowers. The roads, which wind up and down the hillsides to the walls of the Holy City, are teeming with pilgrims. It is Friday afternoon and the great Festival of the Passover starts at sundown. Tomorrow is a doubly holy day since it is also the Sabbath, the Jewish Sunday, when no work, and that includes travelling, is allowed. There is a last minute rush to complete what has to be done; pilgrims are arriving late trying to find somewhere to stay or camping in the surrounding hillsides; the last of the lambs for the festival meal are being slaughtered at the temple.

A small group of women, the relatives and followers of Jesus, are hurrying from the Crucifixion as light is fading. They are distressed and exhausted with the stress of the day. They have seen their loved one put to death in a horrible way and the body rushed to a nearby tomb under the guidance of the kindly Joseph of Arimathea and Nicodemus. Now there is tomorrow to get through, to weep quietly during the Holy Day, awaiting the time when the burial formalities can be completed.

The next day, Holy Saturday the Sabbath, is quiet. The roads and streets are empty. It is the time of prayer and religious thanksgiving with each family together in its own little group. The Sabbath ends at night fall and so Mary Magdalene and another woman set out for the tomb as early as they can in order to anoint the dead body and perform the last funeral rites. It is still dark when they arrive, but there is sufficient shadowy light from the full moon to enable them to pick their way along the road and find the tomb.

The stone covering the tomb entrance is large and disc-shaped, and resembling a millstone standing up on end. It rolls in a gutter, rather like a sliding door covering or opening the entrance. Even in the dim light the women at once see that the stone is not in place. In a moment of panic Mary runs back to tell Peter. "They have taken the body and we do not know where they

111

have put it!" she gasps.

It is light now. Peter and John 'the other disciple' run to the tomb to investigate. John the younger of the two outruns Peter and arrives first, but rather than entering he only peers inside through the low entrance. He is from a priestly family and might be defiled by contact with a body, so he holds back. Peter, having no such restraints, bends down and shuffles inside. He knows instinctively that something is amiss. John then wants a closer look and follows Peter inside. There is the square of linen, like a head scarf, still rolled into a strip which has been used as the band to hold the jaw in place. The large sheet, which had wrapped the body, is lying discarded where the body should have been. Having taken it all in, the two men return to the city to make further enquiries whilst Mary, who has followed the two back to the spot, stays by the tomb in tears.

What happens next is one of those things which is almost impossible to describe. Jesus appears to Mary. Mary, shaken by the experience, once again hurries home to the disciples. 'I have seen him!' she exclaims remembering that Jesus during his ministry told that he would return to bring in the Kingdom.

This account of the events may be over dramatic, but it could give some feeling of what happened at the moment the New Church was born. Shock turned to excitement for the followers of Jesus with the realisation that his teaching and promises had not finished with his death. A miracle had occurred. The Kingdom would still start at any moment with Jesus, the Christ, returning to lead those who believed in him. It would be his second coming.

DIFFERENCE IN MEANING BETWEEN JESUS AND CHRIST

The word Christ (Greek) has the same meaning as Messiah (Hebrew). When we talk about 'Christ' or 'Jesus Christ' we mean the resurrected Jesus.

When we say just 'Jesus' we mean the historical Jesus, the man before his death. As an example, it was Jesus who told parables during his ministry and Jesus Christ who lives, and is with us now as that part of God within us at the human level.

So far as the early church was concerned, what happened to the physical body was beside the point. Although Jesus had died he was still taking the Jewish nation into its new spiritual order.

The miracle was not that his execution had been undone, so that he was still walking around as before. The miracle was that his life had not ended in the sense that he was continuing as the Messiah, the Christ. He was the king of the new beginning, or that part of God which is directing the affairs in the world towards the new age.

Peter writing to the persecuted churches around AD 64 says:

Being put to death in the flesh, but come to life in the spirit.

1 Peter 3:18

The Christ was still with them. He was seen by many. That was enough to enable the young church to grow quickly into a massive movement.

There are hundreds of theories and beliefs as to what happened to the physical body of Jesus. But whatever did happen the New Testament is virtually silent on the matter. Certainly there was no 'funny business' or trickery going on. Any deception would have been picked up at once and there would not have been that massive growth of the new church.

Here are three possibilities.

Firstly, that an out-and-out miracle occurred with the physical body rising in one way or another, and Jesus appearing in the same body in which he was crucified.

Secondly, that the spiritual 'power' of Jesus was so great that it 'dissolved' the body. One can think of the lesser power of faith healing and the physical effect that has on the human body.

Thirdly, that there was some simple explanation of why the tomb was empty. What happened to the body could have been generally known at the time by the small group within the early Church in Jerusalem but, because it did not invalidate the Resurrection experiences, it would not have been seen as significant.

Jesus would be returning in 'Clouds of Glory', in the same form as he had just been seen, and his risen body was 'different'. Christ appeared and disappeared, through locked doors, and on a number of occasions was at first sight unrecognisable. He was genuinely the same Jesus they had known but yet at the same time was not.

The fact that there was a real crucified body elsewhere would not have been openly discussed. Those who had not experienced the resurrected Christ and who were doubters would not have understood that the matter was outside normal everyday experience.

What might have happened to account for the empty tomb?

One possibility is that there might have been a slight sign of revival when Joseph of Arimathea and Nicodemus placed Jesus in the cool tomb. Today, even with all our fancy hospital equipment, we sometimes have problems in determining exactly when a person has died. The line between life and death is not always clear.

Perhaps Jesus died on the cross in all senses but still had sufficient physical life in parts of the body for a final slight movement. It would have been enough for Joseph and Nicodemus to rush the body from the tomb back to one of their homes. By that time Jesus would have been absolutely dead and would have had to be buried elsewhere.

But by then the Sabbath had started; they and their servants would have been ritually unclean because they had been in the presence of a corpse. This, as well as the prohibition of travel on the Sabbath would have meant that it would not have been possible to contact the disciples until the next day. By then Mary Magdalene would already have left for the tomb, and the miracle of the Resurrection would have taken place.

What about the other sightings of Jesus? It was not just Mary Magdalene who saw him. According to John he then appeared twice to all the disciples on consecutive Sunday evenings.

The earliest account we have of the Resurrection sightings comes in Paul's letter to those in Corinth in Greece. Although it was written about twenty years after the events Paul says that his account had been handed down to him.

> For I delivered to you first of all that which also I received, how that Christ died for our sins according to the scriptures; and that he was buried; and that he hath been raised on the third day according to scriptures; and that he appeared to Cephas [Peter]; then to the twelve.
> Then he appeared to above five hundred brethren at once, of whom the greater part remain until now, but some are fallen asleep; then he appeared to James; then to all the apostles; and last of all, as unto one born out of due time, he appeared to me also.
>
> I Corinthians 15:3-8

Here is a summary of the sightings mentioned in this letter:-

1.	Peter
2.	The Twelve
3.	Over five hundred at once
4.	James
5.	All the apostles
End.	Even appeared to me

All the four gospels agree that Mary Magdalene was at the tomb when the risen Jesus was seen. But reading this letter from Paul you would not think a woman was present. Why? Because in those times women's evidence might be thought to be the cause of doubt, and to make his case stronger, it is very likely that Paul gave the privilege to Peter. Peter was well known and respected as the leading disciple of Jesus and there could have been no question then that it was 'just silly women's gossip', especially as the position of women in society was not the same as it is today.

Paul is a fascinating character; intelligent, persuasive, excitable and much like the good politician of today. He had that passion to carry out the cause in which he so much believed; it was the work which God had planned for him. We have no other record than Paul's letter of the appearance to 'over five hundred at once' although it could refer to the giving of the Holy Spirit on the day of Pentecost told in Acts 2:1-41. Likewise we know little about the appearances to the individuals, James and 'all the apostles'.

JAMES AS HEAD OF CHURCH

After reading the gospels it comes as a shock to find that James, Jesus' brother, became the head of the church. In the gospels he is barely mentioned and we get the impression that Jesus' family was not happy with what Jesus was doing. Paul tells us in 1 Corinthians 9:5 that Jesus' brothers, together with their wives, were travelling in the ministry and were part of the church.

Paul says that he was the last to see Jesus. This sighting was at the time of Paul's conversion as he was going to Damascus to arrest any who followed the new way, take them to Jerusalem for trial and maybe death. He saw a blinding light and heard Jesus speaking to him. The incident is described in Acts 9:1-9. Even if the facts of Jesus' appearances which Paul tells are not in line

115

with the gospels, they do indicate that the appearances were fairly widespread.

What did meeting Jesus mean for Paul? It meant a complete change in his direction of life. It meant that from that time on Jesus the Christ was part of his spiritual being as well as part of the whole Christian movement. He was, as one might say, in communion with the Christ as well as everything going on in the new church. It was not an experience of seeing the living body of someone you thought dead, but of being at one with that risen Jesus and all that Jesus taught.

Although Paul said that he was the last to see the risen Jesus, he was not strictly right. Jesus has been seen throughout the ages and sightings or experiences of his presence occur today, even for those you would think unlikely candidates. A highly spiritual Quaker and not the sort of person who would expect to be aware of the presence of Jesus had such an experience. She wrote in her spiritual biography:–

> I have been very fortunate over the years in my prayer companions. During the past few years I have visited a vicar's wife in a neighbouring village, and once a week at nine in the morning we meet for an hour. This weekly occasion has turned into a precious prayer partnership in which we remember the needs of the village, our friends and our families. I am particularly blessed in this friendship because while I am a Light-centred type of soul, my friend is a very Jesus-centred one. Together we enter into one another's experience, and while she sometimes sees Light when with me, several times I have very directly known the presence of Jesus of Galilee. On one of these occasions, Jesus seemed to both of us to be sitting on the third chair in the room, and on another we felt his holy hands laid on our heads in blessing. This for me is a very different experience from that of the Cosmic Christ — much more intimate, personal and human, and teaches me something about the truth known by the evangelicals.
>
> Damaris Parker-Rhodes

So the young church grew because of these experiences of the living Christ, and because of the belief that the Kingdom of God was approaching with the spiritual Jesus leading them until the change came.

Although the journey to the new age had started they were not

116

sure exactly how it would be in the future. That was in the hands of God. The gospel writer John tells us this in his letter to the churches written sometime between AD 65 and 100.

> Behold, now are we the children of God, and it is not yet made known what we shall be in the future. We know that, when he shall come, we shall be like him; for we shall see him even as he is.
>
> 1 John 3:2

As we have seen previously in chapter 5 the Kingdom was not just some spiritual idea, but would be very much like this world yet without the nasty bits. It would be similar to the Garden of Eden before the fall of Adam and Eve. John and others close to him believed that this new time would come before John died.

> This saying therefore went forth among the brethren, that that disciple should not die: yet Jesus said not to him, that he should not die; but, "If I wish that he will wait until I come, what is that to you?"
>
> John 21:23

The words used and the style of the writing in this last chapter of the gospel are not quite the same as the rest and it could well have been written not long after John had died around AD 100.

You will have noticed how the Resurrection stories seem disjointed and do not flow easily from one to the next. It is much simpler to write about worldly affairs —history or people's lives— than spiritual or mystical happenings. The worldly affairs can be written in blocks of different things happening, such as meeting someone or how you felt on a special occasion, and the blocks can easily be made to link together as one thing leads to another.

When describing a series of mystical experiences there is little to connect them together because they do not follow on in a logical way. They seem just to happen in ordinary everyday life for no apparent reason. Quite often they do not start suddenly; one only recognises that an experience is occurring when it is well under way. It happened like this to the two disciples on the way to Emmaus as told by Luke in the last chapter of his gospel.

These religious experiences 'just happen' to anyone, including the very young, and feel as though something from outside is acting upon one. They are very personal and very difficult to describe.

We must not dismiss the Resurrection and afterlife just

117

because they are outside our earthly physical time frame. We need to have the humility to realise that we do not understand the workings of non-worldly events. In a strange way this is what belief is about. John wrote his gospel in order, as he sums up at the end, 'that you may believe that Jesus is the Christ': that the death of Jesus was not the end.

In this book we have followed John and his description of the events leading to the Resurrection. We have seen how the synoptic gospels can be split up and re-arranged giving additional credibility to John's account of Jesus' life. A life which is real and believable: a life showing a true human with doubts and disappointments. A human with successes and failures even to the extent of having to go into hiding toward the end. Yet Jesus was a man spiritually massive and powerfully attractive in word and healing deeds. A man so close to God that he was the *Logos*, the Word, the Messiah, not destined to fight wars but to tell of the spiritual world 'above', and 'that believing you may have life in his name'.

EPILOGUE

LIVING IN THE LIGHT

We started by understanding that there are two aspects of God: 'God the Father' in control outside us, and 'God the Spirit' which might be described as a wordless sense of power, love or awe.

Now we have another aspect. That of God in the life on earth. God in the life of Jesus as a person. God in the life of the apostles, disciples, the early church and all humanity. It is the real world including all its imperfections of hate and misery as well as its beauty and happiness.

The use of words, and in particular religious words, can cause so many problems. Even a simple sentence can convey many different meanings and feelings in each of us. But for me, these three aspects of God are a reflection in my mind of the Trinity. That difficult concept to grasp, of God in three separate ways yet God in one. Father, Son and Spirit.

It is all too easy to make theological points and try to define that emotive word 'God'. Instead of looking for proofs and intellectual arguments we need to turn off our reasoning powers and just let the message of the Bible and other spiritual writings seep into us.

John tells us in his gospel that Jesus was clear about one thing, that what matters above all else is the relationship we have with God and others at the innermost level. That is living in the light. It is when we do not live in this light that divisions come between us for we are then putting our own particular way of seeing God in front of the underlying message.

NOTES AND REFERENCES

Page   THE HOLY LAND – MAP (Page x).

x   For discussion on the possible location of Aenon see John Robinson, *The Priority of John* SCM 1985, p.136.

Page   THE MINISTRY OF JESUS – A TIME SCALE (Page xi).

xi   The chart is based on the chronology of John Robinson, *The Priority of John* SCM 1985, p.157 but with modifications and additions. All dates are approximate.

xi   The unnamed festival in (John 5:1) could be the New Year. See Aileen Guilding, *The Fourth Gospel and Jewish Worship* Oxford 1960, p.86.

xi   For date of the Crucifixion see Robert Jewett, *Dating Paul's Life* SCM 1979, p.26ff.

Page   INTRODUCTION (Pages 1–4)

1   The author of the Fourth Gospel is described as John for the sake of convenience and in doing so does not link his identity with any particular person, nor to the fact that more than one person may have been involved.

2   A mass of ancient written material in the Fertile Crescent, from Egypt to Mesopotamia, is available for study, but except for the Dead Sea Scrolls does not tell us directly about Judaism in New Testament times. See James H. Charlesworth, *Jesus within Judaism: New Light from Exciting Archaeological Discoveries* SPCK 1989, and M. Magnusson, *BC:The Archaeology Of The Bible Lands* Bodley Head 1977, for a reviews of archaeological findings.

2   The considerable volume of Jewish Rabbinic literature is post AD 70 and there is debate as to how relevant it is to the first half of the first century.

2   We are the products of our culture and, no matter how much we think we are aware of the influences working on us, we still have to operate within our brain's physical connections which were principally set during the first years of our life. Our ideas of what is going on around us and our expectations influence our perceptions so that we see what we expect to see. At some time most of us have been surprised how wrong an assumption has been when confronted by a statistical evaluation. For example the World Cup football matches owe more to chance than to skill according to Willen Wagnaar (Dutch psychologist whose concern is subjective beliefs about chance), *Independent* 25th June 1990. Another example but at a very basic level is how an optical illusion can distort reality. In the past astronomers interpreted non-existent perceived lines on the surface of Mars as canals. It is only too easy for us today to see 'canals' in the way we perceive the New Testament. We fool ourselves by hiding behind what we think is scientific analysis.

3   John Robinson in *Redating the New Testament* SCM 1975 points to the circular nature of many of the arguments that the New Testament was written late, and many of the assumptions that flow from that. Also see E. P. Sanders, *Jesus and Judaism* SCM 1977, pp.10 & 124.

3   I consider the sound basic theories put forward by a number of authors are spoilt by seeing everything in the light of their theory.

4   I have looked for evidence which would indicate that Robinson's proposal is unsatisfactory but can find little that matches the strength of his arguments. For a comprehensive study see Martin Hengel, *The Johannine Question* SCM 1989.

4   I can think of two main reasons for the lack of popular knowledge of the Johannine chronology. In the first place the simple synoptic chronology is an ideal carrier for the teaching of Jesus. Indeed, there is external evidence it was written for that purpose. Eusebius (AD c260–c339) tells that Papias (AD c130) wrote that Mark was the

interpreter of Peter and wrote accurately but not in order. See *A New Eusebius* SPCK 1987, p.49. As we were brought up on the synoptic chronology our preconceived ideas of Jesus are fashioned by that framework of his life, which then feeds back telling us that the Johannine chronology does not fit our ideas. For example, the proscription of Jesus, when he went into hiding as a wanted criminal at Ephraim (11:54), does not fit well into a simple model of a miracle working saviour. In the second place, the Fourth Gospel chronology is complex with many visits to Jerusalem; it is not easy to unravel as it is interspersed with theological matter.

Part 1 SETTING THE SCENE

Page   1 THE TWO ASPECTS OF GOD (Pages 8-15)

9   In 1964 a Religious Education teacher carried out a survey amongst 15,000 pupils, ranging in age from 11 to 18, in over thirty schools. The schools were of all types, and from different neighbourhoods. He wished to discover how many of the words from (a) The School Hymnal, (b) The Bible and (c) his own vocabulary were understood by the pupils to the extent that they could define them. They had 10 seconds to define each word, this being intended to represent the fact that when people are listening to a hymn, a Bible reading or a preacher they have little time in which to consider the meaning of the words in use. There were 48 words, from ABUNDANT and ADULTERY to WRATH and WROUGHT. Out of a possible 720,000 responses there was a total of only 98 answered definitions. The pupils were obviously trying. For example, only three out of all of the 15,000 children filled in any answers for the word HARLOT, a prostitute. The answers were 'A necklace', 'It's near New York' and 'There was a lady in a castle there once.' Other teachers who were confident that their senior pupils would do much better found that this was not so. Gordon Bailey, personal communication.

11   For summary of split brain studies and references see Walter Wink, *Transforming Bible Study* SCM 1980, also R. Penrose, *The Emperor's New Mind* Vintage 1989. Some art schools use Betty Edwards, *Drawing on the Right Side of the Brain* Fontana 1979.

12   "One can distinguish two ways of approaching God: the way of overcoming estrangement and the way of meeting a stranger" writes Paul Tillich "The two ways symbolise the two possible types of philosophy of religion: the ontological type and the cosmological type. The way of overcoming estrangement symbolises the ontological method in the philosophy of religion. The way of meeting a stranger symbolises the cosmological method." Paul Tillich, 'The two types of Philosophy of Religion' *Theology of Culture*, edited by Robert C. Kimball, Oxford 1959, p.10 and quoted by permission of Oxford University Press. Also Martin Buber, *Two Types of Faith* Routledge 1951.

12. I use the term 'God the Father' as this is the traditional way of perceiving the cosmological aspect of God. My use of the term does not express an opinion as to the meaning of 'Father' when used by Jesus. In today's world with changing family relationships the father is not always seen as a responsible patriarchal figure, and for some it may be a distressing image. I would hope that the readers would select their own images of God.

12   The use of riddles see J. Ashton, *Understanding the Fourth Gospel* Oxford 1991, p.184.

12   The literature on the 'Word', *Logos,* is considerable. See A. E. Harvey, *New English Bible: Companion* Oxford 1970, p.301ff. Although *Logos* was a common word in Greek, John's prologue is saying that the author is using it with external connotations outside space and time, something Stoic philosophers would not understand.

12   It is possible that the author of John is referring to the 'God the Father' aspect of the Spirit in 14:16 ``he shall give you another *Paraclete* that he may be with you for ever, even the Spirit of truth''.

13   Wordless prayer is, and has been, the mainstay of mystics and monastic life.

13   Prayer and the sides of the brain: mantras are a kind of spiritual exercise focusing and quieting the left hemisphere; mandalas focus and quiet the right hemisphere. The great

religious symbols were cultivated by and cultivate **both**.

15 For further discussion on beliefs and aspects of God see Barman, 'Two ways of seeing God' *The Seeker*, Spring 1987, p.26.

Page 2 CONFLICT: NOMADS AND SETTLERS (Pages 16-21)

18 See R. E. Friedman, *Who Wrote the Bible?* Jonathan Cape 1988 for a breakdown of the Old Testament into sections written from cosmic (ontological) and personal (cosmological) viewpoints. Also E. A. Pocock, *Sons of God* Becket 1979.

18 Cedar was exported from 3000 BC. See *A Bible Commentary for Today*, Ed. Howley, Pickering 1979, p.65 and L. Grollenberg *The Penguin Shorter Atlas of the Bible*, (1959) 1978, p.45.

18 The area was forested five hundred years after Abraham. See Joshua 17:14-18. I am not contending that there were no inhabitants in the hill country, but the early main centres of population were in or near the fertile lower ground.

19 Inconsistencies in the Biblical accounts suggest that Abraham may not have been living a semi-nomadic life but he could have been the equivalent of a large land-owning country baron. See Magnus Magnusson, *BC:The Archaeology Of The Bible Lands* Bodley Head 1977, p.39.

19 Quote from Josephus, *Complete Works*, tr. Whiston, 1849, p.738; BJ vi,1,1.

19 Population estimates are most difficult and widely differ. See Stambaugh, *The Social World of the First Christians* SPCK 1986, p.83.

19 Romany Gypsies see *Oxford Junior Encyclopaedia* Vol.1, Oxford 1948, p.212.

21 Those who could not read the scriptures may have been thought lacking in piety. P. Henry, *New directions in New Testament Study* SCM 1979, p.73.

21 The temple in Jerusalem was not the only temple. There was another small temple in Egypt, See Josephus, *Complete Works*, tr. Whiston, 1849, p.782; BJ vii,10,2.

Page 3 THE JEWISH WAY (Pages 22-27)

22 How the writings of The Pentateuch were brought together and dates are not universally accepted. Explanation of this account see R. E. Friedman, *Who Wrote the Bible* Jonathan Cape 1988. The traditional view:- 'J' = Judah, c950 BC; 'E' = Northern Kingdom, post 'J' pre 722 BC; 'D' = found in temple 621 BC, date between 750 - 621 BC; 'P' = Exile to post exile, forms the framework for the whole.

23 Different images of God in the Old Testament. Doctor- Jer.30:17; Nurse- Isa.1:2; Potter- Jer18:6; Silversmith- Mal.3:3; Cleaner- Isa. 4:4; Cheese maker- Job 10:10; Shepherd- Psalm 23; Mother- Isa. 66.13, Deut.32:18; Friend- Jer.3:4.

23 Example of duplication of texts:- Creation- Gen. 2:4b-25 & 1:1-2:3; Ten commandments - Exodus 20 & Deut. 5; Flood - Gen. 6:5-8 &7:8-9,11.

23 See R. E. Friedman, *Who Wrote the Bible?* Jonathan Cape 1988 for list of passages in the Old Testament written from cosmic (ontological) and personal (cosmological) viewpoints. Also E. A. Pocock *Sons of God* Becket 1979.

25 For Good Samaritan see Luke 10:30-37; comments on corpse-impurity and Good Samaritan E. P. Sanders, *Jewish Law from Jesus to Mishnah* SCM 1990, p.41; priests and corpse-impurity Leviticus 21.

26 For a more detailed summary of the Jewish groups see Christopher Rowland, *Christian Origins* SPCK 1985, p.68.

26 Quote from Josephus, *Complete Works*, tr. Whiston, 1849, p.1; V 2.

27 Sacrifices and temple see James Dow, *Collins Gem Dictionary of the Bible* Collins 1964; I. Epstein, *Judaism: A Historical Presentation* Penguin 1970, p.25.

Page 4 THE FREEDOM MOVEMENT (Pages 28-33)

28 For summary of the Jewish feasts see C Rowland, *Christian Origins* SPCK 1985, p.41ff.

28 Further information on Passover *Collins Dictionary of the Bible*, p.439.

28 For possible origin of the use of unleavened bread see B Malina, *The New Testament World* SCM 1981, p.151.

28 Lighting of candles see C Rowland, *Christian Origins* SPCK 1985, p.42 n.8 (p.335) also WM Clow, *The Bible Reader's Encyclopaedia and Concordance* Collins.

29 See also Second Book Maccabees for description of persecutions.

31 For information on the Zealots see Martin Hengel, *The Zealots* 1961 Revised English Edition 1989 Trans. David Smith, T.T.Clark Edinburgh. In a foreword to this translation Hengel explains that, in the intervening years since first publication, archaeological and other evidence have not caused him to change his findings. See chapter 2 for discussion of the names used for the religious fanatics.

32 'Is it lawful to pay taxes to Caesar?' Mark 12:13-17

Page 5 THE ESSENE COMMUNITY (Pages 34-43)

34 How many of the scrolls were written at Qumran is an open question. It is likely that there were many other communities where religious texts were copied, in Jerusalem and elsewhere.

34 The impact of the Qumran finds on many aspects our understanding of Judaism of the time is considerable. See James H. Charlesworth, *Jesus within Judaism: New Light from Exciting Archaeological Discoveries* SPCK 1989,

35 Ritual washing see Geza Vermes, *The Dead Sea Scrolls: Qumran in Perspective* Collins 1977, p.94.

35 The information about Qumran from a number of sources including personal observation.

37 Quote from Josephus, *Complete Works*, tr. Whiston, 1849, p.615; BJ ii,8,3.

37 For life at Qumran see Geza Vermes, *The Dead Sea Scrolls: Qumran in Perspective* Collins 1977.

38 Scroll dualism see J. H. Charlesworth, 'A Critical Comparison of the Dualism in 1QS 3:13-4:26 and the "Dualism" in the Gospel of John', *John and the Dead Sea Scrolls* New York 1991, p.76ff.

38 For the organisation and community rule see 1QS 8 & 6.

39 Origin of Essenes see Geza Vermes, *The Dead Sea Scrolls: Qumran in Perspective* Collins 1977, p.151.

39 Essenes priests see E. P. Sanders, *Jewish Law from Jesus to the Mishnah* SCM 1990, p.37.

39 Quote from Josephus, *Complete Works*, tr. Whiston, 1849, p.615; BJ ii,8,4.

40 For sect numbers see Josephus, *Complete Works*, tr. Whiston, 1849, p.484 for 4000 Essenes and p.460 for 6000 Pharisees; AJ xviii,1,3 & xvii 2.

40 Some Essene communities living normal lives see Geza Vermes *The Dead Sea Scrolls: Qumran in Perspective* Collins 1977, p.97.

40 Sabbath observances are listed in scrolls CD 10 & 11. For full text see Community Rule 1QS 3. *The Dead Sea Scrolls in English*, Tr. G. Vermes, Penguin 1987.

40 Arguments for annual gathering at Qumran see Geza Vermes *The Dead Sea Scrolls: Qumran in Perspective* Collins 1977, p.107.

41 In the last days going into wilderness. Manual of Discipline, 1QS 8.

Page 6 ABOUT THE GOSPELS (Pages 44-55)

44 For summary authenticity of Pauline letters see Christopher Rowland, *Christian Origins* SPCK 1985, p.203

46 The suggestion how the gospels came to be written is speculation but the background against which they were born was dynamic with much movement between the various communities.

47 Oral tradition: see Sanders & Davies, *Studying The Synoptic Gospels* 1989, p.138ff.

47 Many could read although not so many could write: see Alan Millard, Archaeological International Congress on Bible Archaeology, Jerusalem 1984, *The Jerusalem Post*, 6 April 1984.

48 John Robinson, *Redating the New Testament* SCM 1975, suggests that as there is no reference to the fall of the temple in the gospels that they were completed before AD 70.

49 For motorcycling as poetry see Robert Pirsig, *Zen and the Art of Motorcycle Maintenance.*

51 Banks and the way cash was handled in New Testament times see J. Stambaugh, *The Social World of the First Christians* SPCK 1986, p.72.

51 Essenes called themselves Children of Light or Sons of Light. e.g. see CD13, 1QS3; Prof. David Flusser, International Congress on Biblical Archaeology, reported *Jerusalem Post* 6th April 1984.

53 Hebrew was practical language. See:- D. Cupitt, *Sea of Faith*, p.58; S. Cook, *An Introduction to the Bible* Pelican 1945, p.82; example of God loving the successful, Malachi 1:2-3 "Yet I loved Jacob and I hated Esau."

54 Amen. From Hebrew into Greek via the LXX. *Shorter English Dictionary* Oxford. Translations of Amen used by Jesus from RSV, AV, Good News, Jerusalem, Marrow, Knox from Vulgate, NEB. For comments on Amen see John Robinson, *The Priority of John* SCM 1985, p.309.

55 Humour of Jesus see Elton Trueblood, *The Humor of Christ* Libra Book, Longman 1965.

Page   7 THE SYNOPTIC GOSPELS AND JOHN (Pages 56-63)

56 How do we know that it is God talking to us and not just in the mind? This raises the question whether God exists or not and is another matter. If one does not have an understanding of God, even ontologically (see chapter 1), then any further linguistic arguments will not resolve the matter.

57 G. C. D. Howley, *A Bible Commentary for Today* Pickering 1979, p.1142 gives a breakdown of verses in the synoptic account.

57 There are about 250 verses in 'Q' (parallel passages from Matthew and Luke).

61 Martin Hengel, *The Johannine Question* SCM 1989 and John Robinson, *Redating the New Testament* SCM 1975 suggest that the Fourth Gospel evolved over a lifetime, but differ over the date of publication.

61 See John Robinson, *The Priority of John* SCM 1985, p.304 for description of John being likened to a drama.

62 It would not be out of place for Jesus to make regular visits to the temple since Jews, and in particular the religious leaders, were expected to go to the temple in Jerusalem three times a year for the three major festivals— Passover, Dedication and Tabernacles. See chapter 4 for details of the major feasts and obligation in Exodus to visit the temple during the Feasts.

63 The view that the chronology of John should have priority is not new. J. B. Lightfoot *Biblical Essays* 1893 stated that John is the authority for the chronology of the ministry. See also Ernest Renan, *Life of Jesus,* 1863 and John Robinson, *The Priority of John* SCM 1985, p.125.

63 A number of authors state that John changed the chronology to suit his narrative. Equally well the author of the Fourth Gospel could have built his narrative around the chronology. For objections to displacements see Barnabas Lindars, *The New Century Bible Commentary* London 1972, p.48ff.

Page   8 THE GOSPEL OF JOHN (Pages 64-71)

65 The Fourth gospel contains 878 verses of which roughly 745 (85%) have no parallel in the other gospels. About one third (242 verses) can be discounted as not being sayings and happenings of Jesus but the author explaining his theological view, mainly in the prologue and discourses. This reduces the proportion of unique material to about 80%. i.e. 503 unique and 636 total verses when the discourses are completely ignored.

65 That the author of the Fourth Gospel was writing to correct the chronology of the synoptic accounts seems most likely but the opposite point has been stated by many

scholars. I can see no reason why teaching material which was the base for the synoptic gospels would not have been widely available in one form or another at the time. For a useful summary of the problem of establishing the life of Jesus see C. Rowland, *Christian Origins* SPCK 1985, p.126ff.

66 John the Baptist not being the Messiah is mentioned 20 times:- John 1:6-8, 15, 23, 26-28, 29, 31, 32-33, 35, 40, 46; 3:27-28, 28, 29, 30, 31a, 31b, 36; 5:32-34, 36; 10:41. This does not include the times when it is stressed that Jesus is the Messiah as in 14:6 and 20:31.

67 If the chronology of the Fourth Gospel is credible and if the chronology of the synoptic gospels is unreliable, then we have to accept the Fourth Gospel's event sequence since it is all that we have. It is like accepting a Shakespeare play as historical fact assuming we had no other historical records of England's monarchs. See Barman, 'According to the Gospel of John', *The Seeker*, Spring 1992.

70 The decision is yours. John's dualism allowed free human choice. See J. H. Charlesworth, 'A Critical Comparison of the Dualism in 1QS 3:13-4:26 and the "Dualism" in the Gospel of John', *John and the Dead Sea Scrolls* New York 1991, p.76ff.

70 'Life Eternal' see J. Ashton, *Understanding the Fourth Gospel* Oxford 1991, p.217.

71 For background to the Wisdom literature see J. Crenshaw, *Old Testament Wisdom: An Introduction* SCM, 1981. Wisdom being in heaven and covers the earth see Ecclesiasticus 24:3.

71 The Word. See note for page 12. *Logos* is masculine and *Sophia* feminine.

PART 2 THE STORY OF JESUS AS TOLD BY JOHN

Page   9 JOHN THE BAPTIST (Pages 74-79)

75 John the Baptist figures prominently in the New Testament. Matt. 3:1-17, Mark 1:2-15, Luke 3:1-22, John 1:6-36 Acts 1:5.

76 Reed or Reed-beds blowing in the wind. Matt. 11:7 Luke 7:24 Perhaps meaning a man as feeble as a reed. A. E. Harvey, *Companion to the NewTestament* Oxford, p.52.

76 Was the Baptist an Essene? The fact that the Baptist clearly stated that he was not The Prophet (John 1:21), yet fulfils that role as revealing the Messiah, might have occurred if he considered the Essene 'Teacher of Righteousness' as the final prophet. This is speculative since it is conjecture that the Essenes thought that 'The Teacher' was The Prophet.

76 Part of the appeal of John the Baptist could have been that he was mediating God's forgiveness to the poor who were born with physical defects. If Leviticus was interpreted strictly by the temple authorities many poor might have been effectively disenfranchised from the temple. In Leviticus there is an allowance for poverty (5:7-13) when making a sacrifice for an unintentional sin offering (4:27) (i.e. for breaking a religious Law or the purity code by mistake). But there is no mention of an allowance for poverty when making an unintentional guilt offering (5:14 - 6:7) (i.e. for cheating or not paying temple dues by mistake). This guilt offering probably applied to those with congenital deformities since it was thought that defects arose from some past misdeed of the parents (see John 9:34), e.g. not paying taxes to the temple.

77 Josephus tells us that King Herod, fearful of the power of the Baptist's rhetoric to incite, had him executed. Josephus, *Complete Works*, tr. Whiston, 1849; AJ xviii 5,2.

77 Some wondered if John the Baptist was the re-incarnation of Elijah (Mal 4:5,6), the 'prophet of prophets' who lived over 800 years beforehand (1 & 2 Kings). John 1:21.

77 What will happen to the wicked? See 1 QS 4.

78 The Messiah will baptise with the Holy Spirit. John 1:33, Matt. 3:11 Mark 1:8. The Dead Sea Scrolls state that God at the time of visitation will cleanse with the spirit of holiness; like purifying waters: 1 QS 4. See John Robinson, *The Priority of John* SCM 1985, p.175 and A. R. C. Leaney, 'The Johannine Paraclete and the Qumran Scrolls', Ed J. H. Charlesworth, *John and the Dead Sea Scrolls* New York 1991, p.49ff.

78　There are indications that John's first chapter originally started with a fuller account of what happened. At a much later time it was edited and the prologue, the first 14 verses which have inspired so many people for nearly two thousand years, was added. A hint of the rewriting occurs when John the Baptist says at the beginning of the chapter: "This was he of whom I said .." John 1:15 suggesting that there was some dialogue beforehand in the original text which could have been cut out to make room for the prologue. See John Robinson, *The Priority of John* SCM 1985, p.159.

79　John the Baptist denies that he is the awaited prophet (John 1:21) yet fills the part of the prophet in revealing the Messiah. Was this because he was an Essene who could have thought that the Teacher of Righteousness was that prophet? Or was he denying the role because to claim it would be unacceptable to the delegation from Jerusalem, yet 'prepare the way' (Isaiah 40:3) claimed nothing?

79　The tradition that the unrevealed Messiah was even unknown to himself comes from Justin Martyr who died in AD 165, *Dialogue with Trypho* 8.4.

79　'Lamb of God'. See A. E. Harvey, *Companion to the NewTestament* Oxford, and C. H. Dodd, *Interpretation of The Fourth Gospel* Cambridge 1953, p.269f for review of possible origins of the phrase; i.e. Paschal lamb, sin-offering lamb, mistranslation of Aramaic 'ervant', or horned lamb of Jewish apocalypse.

Page　　　　10 JESUS AND THE BAPTIST (Pages 80–86)

81　For a summary of baptism traditions see Ian Wilson, *Jesus the Evidence* Channel 4 1984, p.84. and Morton Smith, *Jesus the Magician* Gollancz 1978, p.98ff.

85　The cursing of the barren fig-tree. See John Robinson, *The Priority of John* SCM 1985, p.130 n.17.

86　An alternative explanation of the temptation is that it could have been a training time with the ministering angels. See E. A. Pocock, *Sons of God* Becket 1978, p.76.

86　Temptation chronology see John Robinson, *The Priority of John* SCM 1985, p.187.

86　The *poor* and the *poor in spirit* were terms which the Essenes described themselves. Some of Jesus' use of the term *poor* could have been associated with those living religious lives. See James H Charlesworth, *Jesus within Judaism* SPCK 1989, pp.68-70.

Page　　　　11 TO GALILEE AND THE KINGDOM (Pages 87–90)

87　"Repent, the kingdom of heaven is at hand" Matt. 3:2.

87　For detailed comments on the story of the Samaritan woman see John Robinson, *The Priority of John* SCM 1985, p.134 note 38, A. E. Harvey, *Companion to New Testament* Oxford 1973 and also A. N. Wilson *Jesus*, 1992, p.153ff.

88　For information on the Samaritans see J. A. Montgomery, *The Samaritans*, 1907 New York 1986, p.xix; R. J. Coggins, *Samaritans & Jews* Oxford 1975, p.87; Magnus Magnusson, *BC:The Archaeology of the Bible Lands* Bodley Head 1977, p.210. There are still Samaritans on Mt. Gerizim, Quaker Peace & Service, Middle East Section, Jan. 1994.

89　Temple destruction and rebuilding. See E. P. Sanders, *Jesus and Judaism* SCM 1985, p.72ff. The tradition may have a simple origin. Had the temple authorities following the cleansing incident argued that without them the temple activities would cease, Jesus could have responded that it would only take 3 days to fetch the rival Essenes from Qumran.

90　There was considerable activity in Samaria showing that the ministry was not confined to followers of the temple cult: Acts 8:5,14-17. The John mentioned in Acts may have been John Zebedee even if he were not the author of the Fourth Gospel.

90　Much of the teaching material probably originates from the time in Galilee.

90　The Fourth Gospel does not state for which Feast Jesus went to Jerusalem (John 5:1). Tabernacles is the more likely as Dedication in mid-winter probably would be too cold for the sick to be lying outside. See note for page xi suggesting that the healing took place at New Year. Also John Robinson, *The Priority of John* SCM 1985, p.138.

90　Although the chronology is sketchy during the time in Galilee, the synoptic and

Johannine event sequences of the time spent in Galilee are similar. See John Robinson, *The Priority of John* SCM 1985, p.191 i.e.:-
1. Cross Sea of Galilee; 2. Feeding; 3. Disciples re-cross lake; 4. Walks on water; 5. Jews ask for a sign; 6. Teaching about bread; 7. Jesus tests disciples' faith; 8. Forewarns of betrayal and death.

Page   12 PROCLAIM HIM KING (Pages 91-95)

91   Death of John the Baptist is not recorded in John but in Matthew 14:6-12 and Mark 6:17-29. John the Baptist's ministry, although very successful, was probably short. See John Robinson, *The Priority of John* SCM 1985, pp.136 & 139.

92   Desert feeding numbers: Matt. 15.38 = 4,000; Matt. 16:9&10 = 5,000 & 4,000; Mark 6.44 = 5,000; Mark 8:9 = 4,000; Luke 9:12 =5,000: John 6:10 = 5,000. For feeding of 5,000 see 2 Kings 4:42-44.

92   Quote from Josephus, *Complete Works*, tr. Whiston, 1849, p.651; BJ iii 3,2.

93   See John Robinson, *The Priority of John* SCM 1985, pp.200-211 for arguments and implications for pressure on Jesus to assume the role of an insurrectionist. The successful return of the Twelve (Luke 9) —and/or the seventy (Luke 10)— proclaiming the kingdom heightened expectations. Speculation that a rising did take place in Jerusalem and that it was put down by a blood bath (Luke 23.12) fits well.

93   Jesus fleeing to Gentile territory. John Robinson, *The Priority of John* SCM 1985, p.141.

94   Temple rulers. Acts 5:33 gives an indication of the Pharisaic influence in Jewish affairs, but it is unlikely that the situation was simple. The administration was probably controlled by an amalgam of Sadducees and Pharisees with complex inter-relationships, although the Sadducees through the chief priests dominated.

94   Jesus avoiding capture. John 10:39.

94   The fact that Jesus was teaching where John the Baptist had been two years before could indicate a continuity between the two movements.

95   It could be claimed that Thomas the Twin was portrayed as being heroic to counter the story of his doubting. If this was so then it could point to an early authorship of the Fourth Gospel since it would not have been necessary to make such corrections had it been composed even in the 70s or 80s which would have been 40 to 50 years later.

Page   13 THE LAST MONTH (Pages 96-104)

97   For background of spirits and demons see G. Vermes, *Jesus the Jew* Collins 1973, p.60 and M. Smith, *Jesus the Magician* Gollancz 1978, p.4.

100 The name Lazarus appears in 'The Rich Man and Lazarus' Luke 16:19-31 and the raising of the dead in verse 31 could suggest a common source with the Johannine material.

100 Jesus and Lazarus condemned see John 11:47-53 and 12:10.

100 Letter of Clement of Alexandria see M. Smith, *The Secret Gospel* Harper 1973. I consider that Smith's contention that the Johannine account was taken and expanded from the Secret Gospel is too simplistic. There is no reason why both could not have come from separate sources, with John writing up the account into narrative. Also see John Robinson, *The Priority of John* SCM 1985, p.221.

100 I. M. Lewis, *Ecstatic Religion* Pelican 1971 gives many examples of trances and possession. Peter in a trance Acts 11:5 and Paul Acts 22:17.

101 For an analysis of the role of the Sanhedrin and of the religious council see E. Rivkin, *What Crucified Jesus* SCM 1984, p.18.

101 For proscription background drawing on Rabbinic sources see John Robinson, *The Priority of John* SCM 1985, pp.223-229.

101 For notes about Ephraim see John Robinson, *The Priority of John* SCM 1985, p.145 n.61.

102 The triumphal entry could have been a corrective measure to a misconceived uprising, or it could have been a planned demonstration by Jesus of his purpose. The synoptic tradition (Mark 11:1) points to the latter and indeed palms pictured on tombs of that

period suggest that palms were symbolic of the afterlife. Maybe it was to demonstrate his non-belligerent message in any subsequent trial before Pilate.

102 The synoptic last supper was a Passover meal, but not so in John.

103 The synoptic accounts also symbolise the last supper as the messianic banquet. Matt. 26:29 = Mark 14:25.

Page   14 KINGDOM NOT OF THIS WORLD (Pages 105-110)

105 The arrest. It is clear from John 18:3 that temple authorities were responsible for the arrest and the order of the words 'cohort' and 'officers' implies strength of the force rather than responsibility for making the arrest. For details of the arrest see John Robinson, *Priority of John* SCM 1985, p.238ff. and C.K. Barrett, *The Gospel According to St. John* SPCK 1978, p.520.

105 'fell to the ground' John 18:6. The number of armed Roman soldiers need not have been great. Soldiers were vulnerable from behind, even from thrown stones, so when on guard they came together into a formation with their shields pointing outwards. Today an officer will command his soldiers to 'fall out' from their formations and John could have been referring to that in a similar way. Barrett states *Chamai* is peculiar to John in the New Testament (9:6 & 18:6). It means 'on the ground', and is used in place of *chamaze* 'to the ground'. Spitting (9:6) 'on the ground' *Chamai* or dropping (in the sense of resting rather than letting go) a shield or spear butt 'on the ground' *Chamai* makes better sense here than 'to the ground' *chamaze*. The statement 'fell on the ground', which might be translated 'to fall out', could have been one of the Johannine phrases written specifically with a deeper theological meaning. Today we sometimes take this deeper meaning of falling and worshipping Jesus as the surface meaning.

106 See E.P.Sanders, *Jesus and Judaism* SCM 1977, ch.6 for difficulties of specifying the reasons for the Crucifixion of Jesus; also table fellowship with sinners.

106 Burying the dead Matt. 8:22, Luke 9:60. See E.P. Sanders, *Jesus and Judaism* SCM 1977, p.252ff. for implications of not burying the dead.

106 That the initiative for the trial came from the Jewish leadership is also stated by Peter in Acts 2:23.

107 Barabbas: Luke 23:19. For arguments see M. Hengel, *The Zealots* 1961 Revised English Edition 1989 Trans. David Smith, T.T.Clark Edinburgh, p.341.

107 It is unlikely that John was shifting the blame from the Romans to the Jews. See John Robinson, *The Priority of John* SCM 1985, p.271ff. for comments on this important topic which goes beyond the scope of this writing.

107 Two thousand ringleaders of an uprising being crucified. See Josephus, *Complete Works*, tr. Whiston, 1849, p.612; BJ ii 5,2.

107 There is an account of the trial and death of Jesus in Jewish literature from the 2nd and 3rd centuries: Babylon Talmud Sanhedrin 43a. See John Robinson, *The Priority of John* SCM 1985, p.225 for quote and comment. For summary of the Rabbinic literature see C. Rowland *Christian Origins* SPCK 1985, p.318ff.

107 Nicodemus could have been a member of an influential family. See John Robinson, *The Priority of John* SCM 1985, p.283.

108 That Judas was forcing an insurrection has not been included in the list of suggestions since it is not compatible with the facts as presented by John.

109 'The disciple whom he loved'. It has been suggested that the beloved disciple and perhaps the author John was the son (or relative) of the High Priest and mentioned in Acts 4:5f. See E. A. Pocock *Sons of God* Becket Oxford 1979 ch. 22. Alternatively he could have been a natural or adopted child of the Baptist. Who ever he was, we could think of him as a teenager to whom Jesus, without a family, naturally showed an affection, maybe from a early age.

109 For comments on the burial see John Robinson, *The Priority of John* SCM 1985, p.282.

110 For the problem of naming the twelve and their symbolic nature see E. P. Sanders, *Jesus and Judaism* SCM 1977, p.101. For table of the references to the names of the twelve

see M. Hengel, *The Johannine Question* SCM 1989, p.18.

Page   15 "I HAVE SEEN HIM" (Pages 111 –118)

111 The synoptists tell that Mary Magdalene was accompanied by others which is supported by John 20:2 'We do not know...'. Description of the tomb is based on the Garden Tomb in Jerusalem, which is less likely to have been the location of the original burial than the area covered by the Church of The Holy Sepulchre.

112 It is assumed here that the author of the Fourth Gospel was the disciple Jesus loved, but this is by no means certain even allowing for John 21:24. But it is supported by Polycrates, Bishop of Ephesus, who wrote in the late 2nd century that it was John who leant against Jesus' breast (John 13:35). He also said that John was a teacher and that he died at Ephesus wearing the sacerdotal plate which was worn by the priests. See *A New Eusebius* SPCK 1987, p.138.

112 For discussion on the grave-clothes see John Robinson, *The Priority of John* SCM 1985, p.291ff.

113 In the dating of 1 Peter I have followed John Robinson, *Redating the New Testament* SCM 1975. He concludes that the author was Peter.

114 The form of crucifixion varied greatly —see M. Hengel, *Crucifixion* SCM 1977— hence we have no knowledge of the circumstances of Jesus' death and any suggestions must be only speculation. Generally the victim fainted which was followed by death from asphyxiation from pressure on the lungs. One possibility in the case of Jesus is that the spear thrust (John 19:34) might not have shortened life but prolonged it. The appearance of blood and 'water' could indicate that Jesus had pleurisy where the space between the two layers encasing the lung are filled with excessive fluid. The pleural fluid may have protected the heart from the spear and at the same time the release of fluid might have reduced the pressure on the lungs thus drawing in a small quantity of air. I am grateful to the late Dr. E. Glaser, Ballachulish, for this insight.

114 Had the body of Jesus been removed from the tomb in the futile hope of revival, it would subsequently have had to have been buried elsewhere. The fact that the very early church knew of this would not have detracted from the Resurrection sightings nor reduced the belief in the parousia. It is consistent with the early church not mentioning the missing physical body; they were forward looking and not venerating a past hero figure. The emphasis on the bodily Resurrection came later as a counter to Docetism (belief that Jesus was only an apparition). See B. Lindars, *The New Century Bible Commentary* London 1972 pp.61ff. & 598.

114 Corinthian letters were written about AD 55. See Robert Jewett, *Dating Paul's Life* SCM 1979.

116 Damaris Parker-Rhodes, *The Way Out is the Way In* Quaker Home Service, London 1987, p.103.

117 The gospel and the letters of John were by same author: John The Elder. See M Hengel, *The Johannine Question* SCM 1989. The main thrust of the argument in 1 John 3:2 was anti-Docetic.

117 There is divided opinion as to the date of the addition of the last chapter (21) to the Fourth Gospel. I consider that it is late post-dating the death of the author. See M. Hengel, *The Johannine Question* and B. Lindars, *The New Century Bible Commentary* London 1972, p.618ff. It should be treated, and judged, separately, and is not as reliable as the eye witness attested (21:24) body of the gospel.

118 Besides having had a strange religious experience myself I have been fortunate to hear of the experiences of others as part of The Seekers Association special interest groups.

118 Quotations in text from John 20:31.

129

INDEX